The Electronic War in the Middle East
1968-70

by the same author

THE WAR IN THE YEMEN
THE GREEK CIVIL WAR 1944–1949
THE INDO-CHINA WAR (1945–54):
A STUDY IN GUERILLA WARFARE
THE THIRD ARAB-ISRAELI WAR
THE KURDISH REVOLT 1961–1970
ARAB GUERILLA POWER 1967–1972

(*out of print*)
KOREA 1950–1953
THE ALGERIAN INSURRECTION 1954–62
THE RED ARMY OF CHINA
THE ARAB ISRAELI WAR, 1948
THE SINAI CAMPAIGN, 1956
THE STORY OF THE FRENCH FOREIGN LEGION
THE RED ARMY (OF RUSSIA)
MALAYA: THE COMMUNIST-INSURGENT WAR 1948–60

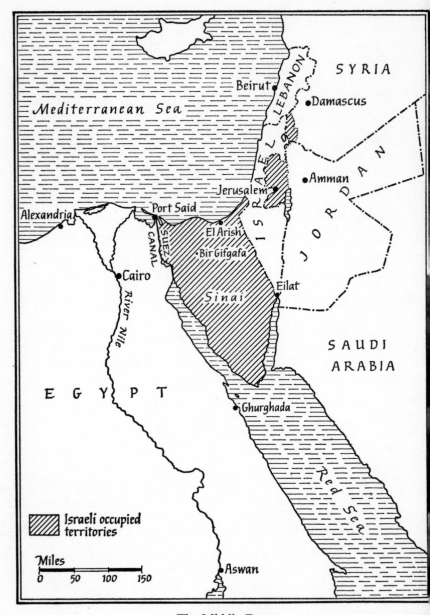

The Middle East

The Electronic War
in the Middle East
1968-70

EDGAR O'BALLANCE

ARCHON BOOKS
1974

First published in 1974
by Faber and Faber, Limited, London,
and in the United States of America
as an Archon Book, an imprint of
The Shoe String Press, Inc.,
Hamden, Connecticut 06514
All rights reserved

© 1974 by Edgar O'Ballance

Library of Congress Cataloging in Publication Data

O'Ballance, Edgar.
   The electronic war in the Middle East, 1968–70.

   1. Jewish-Arab relations—1967–1973.   2. Egypt—
Armed Forces. I. Title.
DS119.7.O24 1974   327.5694'017'4927   74-8965
ISBN 0-208-01469-1

Printed in Great Britain

Contents

7

Acknowledgements

Most of the information I have used in this book has been personally gained by me during briefings, interviews, discussions, and visits to battle fronts and elsewhere. I would particularly like to thank Denis Green for his explanations of the science of electronics. I found the 'What Happened' chronology in the *New Middle East* of considerable help, and I am indebted to that periodical also for the translations of Hebrew and Arabic speeches and documents. Further, I would like to make grateful acknowledgement to the authors, editors, compilers and publishers of the following works, which I have read or consulted with profit and pleasure.

Heikal, Mohammed Hassanein, *Gamal Abdul Nasser*, Doubleday, New York (1972)

Jane's All the World's Aircraft (of various years)
Jane's Fighting Ships (of various years)
Jane's Weapon Systems (of various years)
Keesings Contemporary Archives (of various years)
The Military Balance (various years), Institute for Strategic Studies, London
Strategic Survey (various years), Institute for Strategic Studies, London

Preface

President Nasser's three-year-long war of attrition, lasting from July 1967 until August 1970, in which two super powers, America and the Soviet Union, fought by proxy, testing their sophisticated weapons and counters against each other (although the fighting was mostly done by the Israelis and the Egyptians), was the first electronic war in history. The 'electronic summer' of the war reads like science fiction, with aircraft dodging and diverting missiles as each of the antagonists tried to keep one step ahead of the other, as progressively improved Electronic Counter Measures (ECM) pods and radar detection equipment were supplied. In this highly specialized field of radar-beams, beam-riding, jamming, diverting and counter-jamming, the technicalities are kept down to a minimum and the simplest possible explanation is given so that the general reader who has little or no scientific knowledge or bent can understand what was happening.

To a bemused layman this 'scientists' war' must seem like a magician's war, as electronics came into full play. It has been explained that if equipment needs 'wires' to manipulate it, such as a switch and an electric light, it must be electric, but if it is worked without 'wires' it is electronic—perhaps an over-simplification, but it may suffice. The technically-minded may have liked more precise detail, but in any case many aspects are still classified, so they could not be completely satisfied. Some may say that the war in Vietnam was an 'electronic' one, but it was not quite so as huge ground forces were involved. Electronics played only a minor part, especially on the North Vietnamese and Viet Cong side, and the war did not revolve round them, whereas over the Suez Canal in the latter stages electronics dominated the war. In the electronic war the main ground forces did not clash (although there were many commando raids on both sides), as the Suez Canal effectively kept them apart, and so they have been overshadowed to a certain extent.

It was also a propaganda war and a war of communiqués, when conflicting claims were almost impossible to reconcile. Far more accurate and truthful, the Israelis selectively issued figures, usually to prove or rebut some point, which did not always add up correctly or were out of context, while Egyptian claims were usually so outrageously and patently exaggerated that they destroyed most vestiges of their credibility. I have striven to force apart the veils of heavy propaganda, and what I have narrated is most probably what actually happened.

Neither the Israelis nor the Egyptians could devote their single-minded attention and all their resources to this war. President Nasser, the first Egyptian to rule Egypt for over 2,000 years, was preoccupied with trying to unite the Arabs, or as many of them as he could, under his banner, and their deviousness and intransigence took much of his time and energy, as did his tussle with the Fedayeen. One is somewhat surprised that he allowed his rhetoric to lead him into the electronic war he feared so much, as he thought the Americans would outsmart the Russians. The Israelis were preoccupied on other fronts as well, and with the Fedayeen.

The situation was unusual in history; the defeated Arabs would not come to the same negotiating table with the Israelis, as was customary with victor and vanquished, but blandly ignored their very existence. Another fact not commonly emphasized was that the Egyptians had a huge refugee problem of about 750,000 homeless people, nearly three-quarters as many as the Palestinians, but they were not political pawns and could be absorbed and hidden more easily within Egypt's teeming millions.

The cease-fire came at a vital time, when both were preparing for the still 'unfought round', which both thought they might win. Israeli aircraft had already been pushed out from the Egyptian skies, of which they had had the freedom for so many months, and the Israeli air force could barely venture 30 kilometres west of the Canal. Despite their confidence, unless they had more electronic counters up their sleeves the Israelis may not have come out as well as they anticipated.

While great credit is quite rightly given to the skill and courage of the Israeli pilots, and to the Israelis generally, such qualities when found in Egyptians were frequently ignored, but it should be mentioned that the out-fought, inexperienced Egyptian pilots constantly had a go at Israeli aircraft despite casualties and losses, that gunners in positions along the Canal stood by their guns despite almost constant aerial and artillery assaults, and personnel working frantically to restore the SAM box as it was shattered nightly showed courage and persistence of a high order. Another point often overlooked was that the Egyptian special forces, the commandos, were tough and well-trained and their activities worried the Israelis far more than they would admit.

As this book goes to press the Fifth Arab-Israeli War has broken out and is in progress. This account accordingly will be seen as something of a prelude to a more advanced electronic struggle.

EDGAR O'BALLANCE

1 · President Nasser Survives

'Now the war is over trouble begins'
MOSHE DAYAN

It is an understatement to say that the Egyptians, in common with all other Arabs, were stunned by their sudden and unexpected defeat by the Israelis in the short third Arab-Israeli war[1] of the 5th to the 10th June 1967, which the Israelis know as the Six Day War and the Arabs as the June War. They had been promised, and they never doubted, that victory would be theirs; thoughts of a stalemate, let alone a débâcle, never crossed their minds. Heavy censorship and propaganda kept bad news from the people, who only vaguely began to sense that all was not well on the third day of the war, the 7th, when Radio Cairo stopped its boastful war communiqués and replaced them with readings from the Koran.

By the 8th June Israeli armoured columns, speeding across the Sinai desert, were nearing the Suez Canal, and the Egyptians were in full retreat. By this time senior Egyptian commanders knew exactly how hopeless the situation was. That evening President Nasser conferred with several senior officers, who included Field Marshal Abdul Hakim Amer, Deputy Supreme Commander (Nasser was the Supreme Commander of the Armed Forces), the commanders of the army, air force and navy, and certain other staff officers. During much discussion and argument the generals urged Nasser to resign, but he put them off, ending the conference by saying that he would think the matter over and make a statement to the nation on the following day.

The Israelis were soon on the east bank of the Suez Canal at several points and in the early hours of the 9th a cease-fire came into effect, the Suez Canal being the *de facto* demarcation line between opposing armies. The bulk of the Egyptian air force had been destroyed in a

[1] See *The Third Arab-Israeli War* by Edgar O'Ballance.

15

few hours. The Egyptian expeditionary force in the Sinai, some 90,000-strong, had been defeated and driven back in four days, losing in the process practically all its modern arms, vehicles and equipment so recently supplied by the Soviet Union.

On the 9th June President Nasser made his famous 'resignation speech' on Egyptian television, in which he declared that 'Israel had struck a stronger blow than we expected', and went on to say that 'We cannot hide from ourselves the fact that we have met with a grave setback in the last few days . . . I am willing to assume the entire responsibility . . . I have decided to give up . . . every official post and every political role and return to the ranks of the public'. He nominated as his successor a former premier, Zakharia Moheiddin, a friend of his for years and a fellow member of the group of Young Officers who overthrew King Farouk in 1952. Marshal Amer resigned on the same day, as did Shamseddin Badran, the Defence Minister.

The immediate reaction to the 'resignation speech' was that thousands of people, many in tears, flocked on to the streets of Cairo and other Egyptian cities, loudly demonstrating their support for Nasser and calling on him to remain as head of state. Later that evening the National Assembly, which had no more idea of the enormity of the disaster than had the people, passed a resolution urging Nasser to remain as President. It was only much later, when survivors straggled back from the Sinai and prisoners-of-war were repatriated, that the situation became apparent. Owing to clever propaganda and censorship the total extent of the defeat was never fully appreciated by the Egyptian nation. Many organizations, including the armed forces and the youth section of the Arab Socialist Union (the ASU), the only permitted political party, and numerous prominent personalities addressed appeals to Nasser to stay. Zakharia Moheiddin himself made a brief broadcast in which he said that he could not accept the Presidency, and that the only man to lead Egypt was Gamal Abdul Nasser. This clinched the matter and the following day, the 10th, Nasser announced his decision to remain in office 'in view of the people's determination to refuse my resignation'. Cynical commentators have doubted the spontaneity of the pro-Nasser demonstrations, some suggesting deliberate political planning, stage-management and rabble-rousing, but no really convincing proof has yet been produced to support these insinuations. There can be no denying that at this moment of ignorance Nasser was extremely popular with the masses.

Having settled back firmly in the Egyptian saddle, President Nasser next took action to negate any possible opposition from the defeated and smarting armed forces, which might blame him for the débâcle and try to oust him from power. On the 11th he turned on the senior officers who had advised him to resign four days previously and dismissed eight of them, including Lieutenant-General Mohsen Mortagi, former commander of the Egyptian forces in the Sinai, and Admiral Soliman Izzat, the Commander of the Navy, the others being major-generals in key positions. Also dismissed was Ahmed Said, Director of Broadcasting Services.

The Chief of Staff of the Armed Forces, Lieutenant-General Mohammed Fawzi, considered by Nasser to be capable but not too astute politically, was appointed to the new post of Commander-in-Chief of the Armed Forces to succeed Marshal Amer, whose former post as Deputy Supreme Commander was abolished. Fresh from his defeats in Jordan, Lieutenant-General Abdul Muniem Riad became Chief of Staff of the Armed Forces, and Rear-Admiral Fuad Zaki the Commander of the Navy. All loyal supporters of Nasser, they were in positions to thwart any potential insurrections by discontented officers. Dismissals and arrests of officers were designed to weed out political suspects and strengthen support for Nasser in the armed forces as much as to punish those who had failed in battle.

On the 19th June President Nasser formed a new Government with himself as Premier. At the same time he took over the post of Secretary-General of the ASU. Thus, together with the Presidency, he held the three most powerful offices in Egypt, all political, military and executive power being in his hands. Nasser had certainly survived politically. Mohammed Abdul Wahab el-Bishry was appointed Minister of Defence and Military Production, but he was replaced a month later, on the 21st July, by Amin Howeidi, an ambassador and former army officer.

On the other hand, the military situation was as bad as it could be. The main part of the Egyptian armed forces had been shattered, involving a loss of two-thirds of its 450 combat aircraft, some 800 of its 1,000 tanks and practically all the equipment that had been taken forward into the Sinai. Two armoured and five infantry divisions and 12 artillery units had been scattered and were ineffective, leaving in Egypt only an armoured division in the process of forming, a dozen small commando units, a few training centres and detachments of administrative troops. The only other organized military body was the distant and small Egyptian expeditionary force in the Yemen, which was down to about 15,000 men, as two of its brigades, amounting to about 5,000 soldiers, were in transit back home, having been recalled at the outbreak of the June War. The Israelis had complete control of the air, Egypt was on the verge of military collapse, and there seemed little if anything to prevent the Israelis crossing the Suez Canal and advancing towards Cairo. Nasser later said:[1] 'We had no defences on the west side of the Suez Canal. Not a single soldier stood between the enemy and the capital. The road to Cairo was open. The Egyptian plight was like that of the British at Dunkirk'.

Having lost such huge quantities of Soviet arms and equipment so quickly, the anxious Egyptian Government doubted whether the hard-headed Soviet Union would send it any more, and as the governments of America, Britain and France had been alienated there was momentary despair. There was no need to worry on this score. Already on the 18th June, at a meeting of Arab foreign ministers in Kuwait, the Algerian Foreign Minister said that the Soviet Government had promised Colonel Boumedienne during a recent visit to Russia that the Soviet Union would make good all Arab losses in the June War. To the surprise of many, this proved to be true. On the 20th, little more than a week after the end of the June War, Marshal Zakharov, Soviet Chief of Staff, accompanied by a large Soviet military mission, appeared in Cairo where, apart from two short visits to Syria, he remained for a fortnight. More impressively still, President Podgorny, of the Soviet Union, landed in Cairo on the following day, the 21st, where he spent three days in talks with Nasser.

Although concerned about the material losses in the June War and the blatant Egyptian disregard of Soviet advice on strategy, training and tactics, Podgorny chose to back Nasser rather than any of the other Arab leaders, because the Soviet Union sought to penetrate and spread its influence in the Middle East and into Africa. He openly affirmed Soviet support for Egypt against Israel, agreeing to give financial, economic and military aid, but this time

[1] Speech made on the 22nd November 1967.

18

the Soviet Union intended to keep much stricter control over arms dispatched. President Podgorny was later reported[1] to have said: 'Everywhere we will keep our hands on the key to the arms we are giving them'. On the 10th July a Soviet naval squadron sailed into Port Said and Alexandria harbours to demonstrate Soviet support for Nasser, and also to help deter the Israelis should they be tempted to advance westwards.

Marshal Zakharov's task was to determine the amount of material necessary for the immediate defence of Egypt, to arrange for it to be dispatched and to establish a resident Soviet military mission that would help the Egyptians assimilate it and control its use. On the 25th June the first Soviet plane-load of arms arrived at Cairo West airport, and this was followed at increasingly frequent intervals by others. Within a fortnight some 200 Soviet transport aircraft had landed in Egypt to disgorge crated equipment, mainly of a defensive character—mortars, fields guns and combat aircraft. Few bomber aircraft or long range guns were included. Crated material which had been hastily dispersed to, and stockpiled in, the Yemen during the June War for safety, was brought back to Egypt.[2] Throughout the summer at least two Soviet cargo ships called at Egyptian ports weekly to unload military equipment, until by mid-October it was generally accepted that up to 60 per cent of Egyptian losses in the June War had been replaced. The decision to rearm Egypt amazed many, but it especially dismayed Israel, which noted the promptness and efficiency with which this was being carried out.

So well did the rearmament programme go and so confident did Nasser become that he toyed with a military diversion in the Yemen. During the June War the royalists, fighting against the republicans backed by Egypt, urged Nasser to withdraw his small expeditionary force and use it to fight the Israelis, rather than themselves, saying that if he did so they would not attack the republicans in its absence. Nasser did not reply but instead, on the 5th and 6th, the first two days of the June War, Egyptian aircraft bombed royalists as a warning for them to keep their distance. Piqued, the royalists, who

---

[1] *Time* of the 21st July 1967.

[2] 'Stockpiled for safety in the Yemen, which was out of range of Israeli aircraft ... were at least a hundred Soviet aircraft in crates on the airfields at Hodeida and Sana'. *War in the Yemen* by Edgar O'Ballance.

had Saudi Arabian backing, began an offensive that had some success. Once the June War was over, Nasser had recovered from his fright and Soviet arms were pouring into Egypt again, the Egyptian expeditionary force was reinforced until it had a strength of over 25,000 men, supported by aircraft, guns and armour. Operations were mounted that succeeded in regaining most of the territory so recently lost to the royalists.

A factor of considerable strategic importance was the Suez Canal. Because of allegedly American and British intervention in the June War it had been officially closed by Nasser on the 6th June to ships of those countries, or those trading to or from them. In fact it was made impassable to all shipping throughout the June War owing to Israeli air supremacy and action. On the 11th the Chairman of the Suez Canal Authority announced that the Canal had been closed because the Israelis had sunk several ships in it, but he declined to give names or nationalities. In reality it had been deliberately blocked on Nasser's orders, there being two partly sunken Egyptian 'pilgrim' ships, each of some 8,000 tons, just south of Port Said, two partly sunken floating docks filled with concrete between Ishmailia and the Great Bitter Lakes, and a small, 5,000 ton Egyptian tanker partly blocking the Canal near Port Suez.[1] Also, 15 foreign ships, including four British, were trapped in the Great Bitter Lakes, but most of the personnel on them were evacuated by the Egyptians soon after the June War ended, only skeleton crews remaining on the ships.

Another commodity of considerable strategic interest was oil. On the 6th June the Arab oil states had placed an embargo on all deliveries to Britain and America, which remained in force after the June War, but before many days passed the economic pinch began to be felt. Saudi Arabia was the first to murmur on the 30th June, when in an interview the Minister of Oil admitted that the embargo was hurting his country's economy and that it had lost £11 million in the 24 days so far. On the same day a Kuwaiti newspaper stated that the obligation of fulfilling the embargo caused its Government's revenue to fall by 40 per cent. On the 7th July a statement by the Saudi Arabian Government indicated that there was no longer any reason to continue the embargo on supplies of oil to America and

[1] *The Times* of the 12th June 1967.

Britain as it was now ascertained they were not implicated in the June War. The statement added caustically that the Arab states were not the sole source of oil in the world. But the embargo remained, mainly because of pressure by Syria and Algeria.

On the 12th June, when Tunisia expressed solidarity with Egypt and offered to send Tunisian troops to fight the Israelis, diplomatic relations between the two countries, which had been severed in October 1966, were resumed. On the 15th, President Atassi of Syria flew to Cairo to meet Nasser, and on the following day Nasser went to Algiers to have talks with Colonel Boumedienne. On the 10th July both Colonel Boumedienne and King Hussein of Jordan were in Cairo having discussions with Nasser, and on the 11th they were joined by President Aref of Iraq. On the 13th Premier Zeayean of Syria flew to Cairo to see Nasser, where they were joined by President Ismail el-Azhari of the Sudan. President Gamal Abdul Nasser was back in business as the leading statesman of the Middle East.

This latter round of Arab summit talks in Cairo ended on the 16th July, the communiqué merely saying that the heads of state of Egypt, Syria, Iraq, Algeria and the Sudan agreed 'on steps to eliminate the consequences of Israel's aggression against the Arab countries'. But more meetings were to come, it being proposed to hold one of Arab foreign ministers at Khartoum in the immediate future. Meanwhile the victors waited vainly for the defeated to come to the conference table to discuss a post-war settlement. Already, on the 20th June, Premier Eshkol of Israel had said that he was 'Ready to meet President Nasser, King Hussein and other Arab leaders, at any place at any time in order to hold peace talks', but they did not respond, instead choosing to confer amongst themselves. Also hopefully waiting was Moshe Dayan, the Israeli Defence Minister, who was later reported to have said that he 'expected the telephone to ring at any time during the summer conveying the Arabs' peace terms'.

Arab foreign ministers conferred in secret session at Khartoum from the 1st to the 6th August, ending their meeting with a brief communiqué asserting their determination 'to eradicate all vestiges of Zionist-imperialism on Arab soil'. Press reports indicated their opposition to any form of negotiation with Israel, but on other matters they were not so united. Most were against Algerian and Syrian proposals that a Vietnam-type revolutionary guerilla war should be waged against Israel, while Saudi Arabia, Kuwait and Libya argued against tightening the oil embargo against America, Britain and West Germany, and Tunisia urged more effective diplomatic and propaganda efforts and less sabre-rattling. Oil continued to divide the Arabs, the 'have nots' wanting to enforce their extreme views on the 'haves'. In an effort to reach a common policy the finance and oil ministers of Arab states met in Baghdad from the 15th to the 20th August, but they did not seem to resolve anything, their communiqué merely claiming to have 'achieved a spirit of Arab solidarity'. Oil still did not flow from the Arab states to the West.

Another matter of some contention was the continued, although small, Egyptian participation in the Yemen in support of the republican government against royalists backed by Saudi Arabia, a war that ranged two of the most important Arab countries on opposing sides, if not causing them to fight each other by proxy. Premier Mahgoub of the Sudan took on the role of peacemaker, visiting both President Nasser and King Feisal; on the 24th August he announced that both leaders had agreed to work for a settlement based on the 'Sudan Plan', but no details were disclosed. The Sudan Plan was generally understood to provide for a phased withdrawal of Egyptian troops, the ending of financial and other support for the royalists by Saudi Arabia, and the holding of a plebiscite to determine the future form of Yemeni government.

After a preliminary meeting of foreign ministers to draw up an agenda, a conference of heads of most Arab states, or their representatives, met in Khartoum on the 30th August. A notable absentee was Colonel Boumedienne. The Syrian Premier, representing his country, went to Khartoum, but did not take part in the opening session, instead flying home again the same day. Both Algeria and Syria advocated Vietnam-style guerilla warfare which the 'moderates' were against. When the Syrian Premier arrived home an emergency session of the ruling Baathist Party passed a resolution declaring that 'popular war of liberation was the only way to evict Israeli forces from the occupied Arab lands'.

The Khartoum conference ended on the 3rd September. The main decisions were that the flow of oil to the West should resume, the rich oil states should subsidize Egypt and Jordan for their losses in the June War and Egypt for loss of revenue owing to the closure of the Suez Canal,[1] and all steps should be taken to consolidate Arab military strength. In 1966, for example, the profits from the Canal amounted to about £74 million, of which three-quarters came from oil passing through and some £28 million from subsidiary trade; about 21,250 ships passed through that year. More important and far-reaching, perhaps, were the three principles enunciated, of no recognition, no negotiation and no peace with Israel. Nothing was officially mentioned about the Yemen, but it was assumed that Nasser agreed to a policy of complete disengagement, as he abruptly lost interest in that country after the Khartoum conference. On the 3rd Radio Cairo stated that the Suez Canal would remain closed as long as the promised aid from Saudi Arabia, Kuwait and Libya was received. Previously, on the 26th August, General Odd Bull, head of the UN Truce Supervisory Organization (UNTSO), had announced that both Israel and Egypt agreed to extend indefinitely an agreement to abstain from navigation on the Canal, the exception being the use of Egyptian boats to take supplies to the foreign ships stranded in the Great Bitter Lakes.

On the 3rd September Israeli Premier Eshkol issued a statement noting with regret the decisions of the Khartoum conference, which showed that although Nasser had lost the war he was rapidly winning the peace. The unyielding stance of the three principles of no recognition, no negotiation and no peace, convinced the Israelis that they would have to adopt harder measures to force the Arabs to respect the cease-fire, causing them to abandon a policy of restraint which they had sought to exercise so far and to adopt one of reprisal. A tougher attitude was shown when on the 14th September the Israeli Foreign Minister, Abba Eban, said that the map of the Middle East prior to the 5th June 1967 had been irrevocably destroyed, and that the only alternative to the present cease-fire lines was freely negotiated new frontiers assuring peace and security in the area, but the Arabs still would not respond. On the 10th the Israeli Government stated that if no direct peace talks developed during the UN session (due to commence on the 22nd) Israel would remain in the positions it held since the cease-fire at the end of the June fighting.

[1] A total of £135 million was to be paid annually to Egypt and Jordan (Egypt to have £95 million and Jordan £40 million) by Saudi Arabia, which would pay £50 million, Kuwait £55 million and Libya £30 million.

However, Nasser had not yet quite put his own house in order, and to him a circle of dangerous discontents seemed to hover around Marshal Amer, as many dismissed officers visited him at his house on the outskirts of Cairo. Officers in the armed forces generally were smarting under their defeat, their prestige had suddenly collapsed and many were ashamed to wear their uniforms in public in the capital. Most officers had a deep respect for Marshal Amer who, for example, had conducted the brilliant Ramadan campaign[1] in the Yemen in early 1963, which brought over half that country under republican control. It was suddenly announced on the 4th September, in the newspaper *Al Ahram*, that Marshal Amer and some 50 officers and civilians, including Shamseddin Badran, the former Defence Minister, had been arrested for conspiring to seize control of the armed forces. *Al Ahram* was a daily Cairo newspaper, edited by Mohammed Hassanein Heikal, a friend and confidant of Nasser, and the views and opinions printed in the newspaper were thought to reflect those of the President, so much so that *Al Ahram* was generally regarded as being a semi-official journal.

On the 5th Colonel Salah Nasr, Head of Intelligence, was dismissed, the Defence Minister, Amin Howeidi, assuming responsibility while the department was investigated. Further details were given piecemeal in succeeding issues of *Al Ahram*, that of the 13th stating that both Nasr and Abbas Radwan, who had been Minister of the Interior at the outbreak of the June War, had also been arrested. It was said that together with Marshal Amer and Shamseddin Badran they were to form a 'revolutionary council' with the aim of making Badran the Premier and of restoring Amer to his former post. If Nasser refused these demands, Amer was to have led an armoured brigade on Cairo—but he was arrested the day before this was planned to occur, which the newspaper stated to have been the 26th August.

On the 15th it was announced over Radio Cairo that Marshal Amer had committed suicide the previous day, it being explained that on the 13th, when Generals Mohammed Fawzi and Abdul Riad visited Amer at his home to question him, Amer excused himself, went to the bathroom, and took poison from which he did not recover. There was immediate suspicion that he had been forced to kill himself, but the Government and *Al Ahram* described in precise

[1] See *War in the Yemen*, by Edgar O'Ballance.

detail the sequence and manner of his death. On the 19th *Al Ahram* stated that 149 persons were detained under suspicion of being involved in the Amer plot to seize control of the armed forces.

Additionally, Nasser dealt with those responsible for the Egyptian defeat in the field. On the 25th September it was announced that after investigation by a special committee they would be tried, the first four being brought before a military tribunal on the 30th October. They were all senior air force officers, Mohammed Mahmoud Sidky, the former commander, Gamal Afift, the former Chief-of-Staff, Hamid el-Dogeidy, former commander of the Eastern zone, and Ismail Labib, former director of Air Defence. The indictments were not made public because, it was stated, the information contained in them might be of value to the enemy, and the request to hold the trial in secret was granted.

The Suez Canal was now the clear barrier between the opposing land forces. The exception was a small triangle of swamp, salt marsh and salt lake, spreading round Port Fuad at the northern end on the east bank, which was held by the Egyptians, although movement was extremely restricted because of the nature of the terrain. Otherwise the Israelis were on the east bank and the Egyptians on the west bank along its whole length. It was not long before armed friction occurred. The first clash occurred on the 1st July, but details were not precise as both sides gave conflicting versions. The Israelis claimed that about 120 Egyptian troops in boats crossed the Canal near Ras el-Ish, between Kantara and Port Fuad, and opened fire on Israeli positions along the Canal bank, wounding several soldiers. The Egyptians said that the Israelis had attempted to advance towards Port Fuad, the triangle held by the Egyptians, but had been repulsed with the loss of six tanks. On the 3rd the Israelis admitted the first act of sabotage in the Sinai, when a train was derailed. On the 5th two Israeli officers were killed by mortar fire from across the Canal, and on the 8th, when Egyptians shelled Israeli positions near Kantara, the Israelis admitted five killed and 31 wounded, Israeli aircraft having to go into action against the Egyptian guns.

The Israeli Navy, which had not had much opportunity for glory in the June War, came into prominence on the 12th July, when two of its motor torpedo boats (MTBs) were attacked by two Egyptian MTBs near the Romani Bay, off the northern coast of the Sinai. The nearby Israeli destroyer, *Eilat*, moved in and sank both Egyptian

MTBs. Israeli craft suffered no damage, but the Israelis admitted that eight sailors had been wounded. The Egyptians were silent about the incident.

Friction was generating as both sides brought their weapons right up to the edge of the Canal to bombard the other almost at point-blank range. The heaviest fighting since the June War occurred on the 14th July, when guns and mortars opened up across the waterway in several places, mainly near Kantara, Ferdan, Ishmailia and Port Suez. Each accused the other of starting the firing, and made conflicting claims. The Egyptians said that although the Israelis killed two civilians and wounded others at Ishmailia, they destroyed 14 Israeli tanks and 15 armoured vehicles. The Israelis said that Egyptian fire killed five of their soldiers and wounded 20; that Israeli aircraft had silenced Egyptian guns at Port Ibrahim, just south of Port Suez, and at Port Suez; they dismissed the Egyptian claim to have shot down five Israeli aircraft. The war of communiqués was also hotting up.

In view of complaints from both Egypt and Israel to the UN of incidents along the Suez Canal, the Security Council instructed General Odd Bull, of UNTSO, to make arrangements with the two countries for UN observers to be stationed at points along the Canal. On the 10th July Egypt agreed, as did Israel the following day. It was accepted that a cease-fire should come into being at 2100 hours local time[1] on the 15th July, the day after the barrages had taken place, and that UN observers should take up positions on the following day, but there was a short delay. In fact, firing had already died down and there was a comparative lull for some time. The delay was caused by the problem of communication between the UN observers on opposite banks. Israel had wanted them to have ordinary field radios, but Egypt objected to direct contact and wanted them to communicate back through normal UN channels to New York. Eventually it was agreed that UN observers on both sides should communicate back to General Odd Bull's headquarters in Jerusalem.

On the 17th July four observers took up duty on each side of the Canal, three in positions on the Canal bank and the fourth at the forward command headquarters which, on the Egyptian side, was at Ishmailia, and, on the Israeli side, at Kantara. This number slowly

[1] All times quoted are local time, unless otherwise stated.

increased during the ensuing weeks. The problem of navigation remained unsolved, although on the 3rd August Egypt agreed that both sides should refrain from using the Canal, a proposal Israel had already accepted, the exception being boats supplying the foreign ships trapped in the Great Bitter Lakes. Israel wanted the centre of the Canal to be the cease-fire line, but Egypt claimed to own it all.

Despite the presence of UN observers there were spates of firing across the Canal during September, which usually died down when local cease-fires were arranged by the observers. For example, on the 20th Radio Cairo claimed that an Egyptian civilian had been killed and eight injured when the Israelis shelled Port Suez and Port Tewfik, and that in total so far some 44 people had been killed and 170 injured in the Canal area since the June War. The Israelis denied the shelling, saying that their guns had only fired at Egyptian troop-carrying boats that were attempting to use the Canal. The Israelis had agreed to the Egyptians probing the southern part of the Canal to see if it were possible for the 15 foreign ships to sail out, but when the Egyptians began to move north of Ishmailia the Israelis opened fire, causing a dozen casualties. The following day there was artillery fire across the waterway at Kantara, in which the Israelis admitted that four soldiers were killed and six wounded, but claimed to have inflicted Egyptian casualties. On the 27th there were spasms of shelling south from Kantara to Suez town, and it was several hours before the UN observers could arrange a cease-fire. Both accused the other of commencing the incidents, and both claimed to have inflicted losses on the other.

Other claims, not always substantiated, were made as the propaganda war got under way. For example, on the 4th September the Israelis claimed to have sunk an Egyptian MTB after an exchange of fire near Port Tewfik, but there was no confirmation of this. Neither was there any confirmation of Egyptian claims to have destroyed seven Israeli tanks and an armoured vehicle the next day. Egyptian aircraft occasionally made brief timid appearances; already on the 26th August the Israelis claimed that their anti-aircraft guns brought down one near Bir Gifgafa, some 40 miles east of the Canal, while on the 11th October Israeli fighters shot down an Egyptian MiG-21, about 10 miles east of the Great Bitter Lakes. As incidents continued, on the 1st October Nasser appointed Ali Sabry, one of the four Deputy Premiers, to be Resident Minister in the Suez Canal Zone.

His task was to 'hold the front line', and he was given powers to control people and resources within his area.

During most of the day of the 21st October the Israeli destroyer *Eilat* had been manoeuvring in the region of Romani Bay, almost thumbing its nose at the defences of Port Said, but during this time it had been tracked by Egyptian radar. In the evening it was attacked by two Egyptian Komar Class missile ships, and sunk by Styx missiles; of the 202 personnel on board, 47 were lost and 91 were wounded. Israeli helicopters worked with the aid of flares to rescue sailors from the water. There were conflicting accounts of this sinking. Commander Eroll, of the Israeli Navy, stated at a press conference that four missiles were fired at the *Eilat* at 1730 hours, when it was 13 miles from the Egyptian coast, two of which hit the ship, causing it to list. Two hours later, when it was seen that the *Eilat* was not sinking but only listing, two more Styx missiles were fired, one of which hit and sank the ship, while the other exploded amongst survivors in the water. The Egyptian version, given by Major-General Mustafa Kamal, of the General Staff, was that the *Eilat* was only ten miles from Port Said (Egyptian territorial waters extended to 12 miles), and that it sank where it was first hit by missiles well within Egyptian waters. He declined to give the range at which the missiles were fired, but declared that there were no foreigners in the Egyptian armed forces, meaning that there had been no Soviet personnel on the ship. The *Eilat*, the former British 1,710-ton destroyer HMS *Zealous*, had seen service in World War II before being sold to the Israelis in 1956. The Soviet 100-ton Komar Class missile ships had a speed of about 40 knots and carried a pair of missile launchers, the Styx having a range of about 20 miles.

The Israeli reprisal came on the afternoon of the 24th. It began with a few shells fired into Suez town and harbour and developed into a 'rolling barrage' of heavy mortars, which missed little; fire was directed first at the oil refinery about two miles inland, then on to the second refinery a further mile inland, and then on to a fertilizer plant nearby. UN appeals to stop were ignored and the barrage continued for three hours. When it was over the two refineries had been practically destroyed and the oil tanks left blazing, smoke being visible for over 25 miles, heavy damage had been caused to the fertilizer plant, and harbour installations had been disrupted as well. The two refineries then produced about 5 million tons of Egypt's estimated (6·5 million tons) annual consumption of refined oil, the remaining 1·5 million tons being refined at Alexandria. An indication of the severity of this economic blow was that paraffin rationing was introduced in Egypt on the 7th November. To the majority of people outside the cities paraffin was essential for cooking.

Also, Israeli aircraft attacked Egyptian Komar and Osa Class missile ships in Alexandria and Port Said harbours, where only a few days previously ships of the Soviet Navy had been on a courtesy visit. The result was the Soviet ships quickly returned, and from this time onwards there were invariably a few in these two, and other Egyptian harbours, which effectively debarred the Israelis from attacking them for fear of becoming openly involved with the Soviet Union.

On the following day, the 25th, U Thant stated that he intended to strengthen UNTSO by increasing the number of UN observers from the existing 43 to 90, to double the number of observation posts from nine to 18 on each side of the Canal, to acquire four patrol boats for the use of UN personnel on the waterway, and to have four helicopters, but there was sluggish reaction to these proposals.

By the end of October 1967 the numbness felt after the June War was fast wearing off and Egyptians were recovering from the shock of their defeat, abrasively reacting to Israeli incidents and initiating military activities of their own. Tension was rising, much damage was caused, shelling was on the increase and casualties were mounting. Additionally, Egypt was now faced with a refugee problem, it being reported[1] that already some 350,000 people had been evacuated from towns and villages near the west side of the Canal. Ishmailia, with a normal population of about 100,000, was nearly devoid of civilians, while it was stated that it was intended to evacuate at least half of the 500,000 population of Port Said because of recent shelling. The Israelis had caused yet another, less publicized but none the less real, Egyptian refugee problem, to add to the existing one of the Palestinians.

[1] *New York Times* of the 21st September 1967.

2 · Military Preparation

'There is no better border than the Suez Canal'
Premier LEVI ESHKOL

President Nasser and the Egyptians, having survived the after-math of defeat, and bolstered up by more Soviet arms and open backing, began to develop an aggressive reaction. On the 22nd November 1967 the UN unanimously adopted a British resolution to establish a 'just and lasting peace in the Middle East', which in essence called for the withdrawal of Israeli forces from areas they had occupied since the June War, the Arabs to acknowledge the existence of Israel, a just settlement of the Palestinian refugee problem and the establishment of demilitarized zones. Frequently referred to as the 'November Resolution',[1] or 'Resolution 242', that being its serial number, it immediately became a controversial talking point, and has remained so since.

The November Resolution called for the appointment of a special representative of the UN to go to the Middle East and make contacts with heads of state and others to promote agreement and 'assist efforts to achieve a peaceful and acceptable settlement'. U Thant, the UN Secretary-General, appointed Gunnar Jarring, then Swedish Ambassador to Moscow, but an acceptable settlement was elusive, and Jarring spent weeks and months fruitlessly travelling from country to country and capital to capital.

Nasser's immediate reaction was to make his first bellicose speech since the June War, when on the following day, the 23rd, he addressed the National Assembly. Emphasizing the three principles of the Khartoum conference, of no recognition, no negotiation and no peace with Israel, he added a fourth, that of 'No interference in the Palestine issue which is the legitimate case of the Palestine people'. He said that the Egyptians would not permit Israeli navigation on the Suez Canal. Boastful once more, he went on: 'We need time to

[1] See Appendix B for a complete version.

complete our military preparedness. We can now defend ourselves . . .
if the time comes for military action we will not be on the defensive.
We must choose the time and place'. Claiming that the Egyptian
army was stronger than before June 1967 and that time was on
Egypt's side, he quoted the recent naval action in which the Israeli
ship, *Eilat*, was sunk, as an omen of things to come.

Israeli reaction to the November Resolution and Nasser's speech
was one of dismay, as the fruits of military victory faded, but the
Israeli attitude was equally uncompromising. The Israelis demanded
direct negotiations with the Arabs. On the 12th June and again on
the 30th October 1967 Premier Eshkol stated in the Knesset that there
could be no return to conditions existing before the 5th June 1967,
that a peace settlement could be brought about only by direct
negotiation with the Arab countries concerned, and must include
such matters as the free passage of Israeli ships through the Straits
of Tiran and the Suez Canal. The Israelis insisted that secure
borders could only be within the framework of a peace settlement.
Israel and Egypt were on a collision course, and both looked to their
armed forces in preparation.

By the end of 1967 the scattered formations of the Egyptian army
had been put together again and largely re-equipped with modern
Soviet arms and material. As the best estimate at the time was that
60 per cent of the June losses, amounting to at least (by February
1968) 450 medium tanks, 250 heavy guns and 300 field guns and
mortars, had been replaced, by a rough rule of thumb Egypt possessed about 550 tanks, mostly T-55s, 300 heavy guns, 400 field
guns, 200 mortars of various sorts, and up to 800 light armoured
vehicles, including armoured personnel carriers. This was sufficient
to give the Egyptians the capability and the confidence to hold the
line of the Suez Canal and oppose any attempted Israeli crossing,
but hardly enough to allow the Egyptians to punch their way back
into the Sinai.

The infantry element was reformed into six divisions, of which
three were right forward along the Canal, as was most of the artillery,
batteries being reformed as Soviet guns were received. The three
armoured divisions, each comprising two armoured brigades only
at this stage, were lying back to the west of the Canal behind the
forward infantry divisions. The paratroop brigade and the commandos tended to merge together and be later known as the special

forces, there having been 15 small commando units at the commencement of the June War.[1]

With a population of just over 30 million, increasing by three-quarters of a million annually, and a three-year period of conscription in force, Nasser did not have a manpower problem. The Egyptian armed forces at the beginning of the June War numbered about 190,000, but this figure included a proportion—perhaps as high as one-third—of recalled reservists. The army had been about 160,000-strong, of which some 20,000 were either still in the Yemen or returning from that country, and 90,000 had been sent across the Canal into the Sinai, leaving only about 50,000 military personnel in Egypt proper. As the ratio of 'teeth' to 'tail' in the army was the unexpectedly high one of 40:60, one can appreciate just how defenceless Egypt had been immediately after the June War. The armed forces were backed by an armed 60,000-strong national guard for internal security tasks, and so the total numbers engaged on full-time military duties were only about 250,000—which in a nation of 30 million people was quite small. Losses in the June War had not been heavy, and according to Nasser[2] had been '10,000 soldiers and 1,500 officers lost . . . 5,000 soldiers and 500 officers captured'. Figures of losses tend to vary and seem to have been kept deliberately vague and misleading. Morale was the unknown factor at this moment, and troops returning from the Sinai were segregated in camps in the desert until they had been 'reconditioned' before being fed back into their units, or sent to new units. After the June War more reservists were recalled and more conscripts were called up until the overall strength of the army rose to 190,000, and then even higher.

The Egyptian army tried to get down to reorganizing itself, but was hampered to a degree by purges, over 800 officers—mostly senior—in all being dismissed or arrested, in addition to the some 2,000 lost in the June War, and the release and exchange of prisoners lagged. It was assisted by an enlarged Soviet military mission, which by the new year of 1968 was over 2,000 strong, Soviet advisers being threaded throughout the army right down to unit

---

[1] Only two of which went into action, being sent to Jordan to infiltrate into Israel from that country. Of about 240 men, some 40 were killed and 40 captured, the remainder eventually making their way back to Jordan or Egypt.

[2] In his speech on the 23rd November 1967.

level. The Soviet instructors found the Egyptians difficult to deal with because they were too impatient to appreciate Soviet methods, which were slow, methodical and thorough. At first the role of the Russians was only advisory, but when he detected sluggishness in the Egyptian officer corps, Nasser asked them to take on a larger part of the reorganization and training. Then he ordered all Egyptian officers to obey Soviet advisers, even though they might be junior in rank; some of them complained but all were overruled on Nasser's insistence. This caused friction between the Egyptians and the Russians which did not make for efficiency. The Soviet officers insisted on harder, longer and more varied training, and on the progressive development from merely training individual weapon crews to welding them into cohesive units each with a strong inherent *esprit de corps*. The Egyptian armed forces were frequently visited by senior Soviet officers, and senior Egyptian officers were sent to the Soviet Union for briefings and courses of instruction. In March 1968, for example, Marshal Grechko, the Soviet Chief of Staff, paid a searching fact-finding five-day visit to Egypt.

Both General Fawzi, the Commander-in-Chief, and General Riad, his Chief-of-Staff, were capable and realistic officers, and in the reshuffling of commands and posts they made some good choices. While not as efficient and dedicated as his Israeli opposite number, the Egyptian officer, especially the regimental one, was not as bad as hostile Western and Israeli propaganda had painted him. Before the June War officers had immense prestige, and accordingly there were many applicants, enabling only the best to be selected. After the war they were deprived of many privileges and had to spend their time with their units working hard; there were no more long weekends in Cairo, a practice that had become almost traditional. They felt a smarting sense of chagrin, which as it wore off gave way to a determination to prove their worth. As the Egyptian officers responded to the Soviet insistence that they work and train hard with their men, so did their soldiers respond to them, and many Egyptian officers discovered for the first time what a good soldier the Egyptian fellaheen could become if properly led and encouraged. On Soviet insistence certain officers from wealthy families, or with traditional backgrounds of elegance and ease, were removed and replaced with younger ones more sympathetic to Soviet ideals and methods. Also, on Soviet insistence, a number of senior officers who had been dismissed by Nasser, but who had done well on courses in the Soviet Union, or whose efficiency had come to the notice of the Soviet military mission, were reinstated; this applied especially to senior officers, as the Egyptian army was so short of capable and experienced commanders and staff officers.

The Egyptian soldier was tough and sturdy; with such manpower available, a good selection could be made. Indeed, in the early hours of the June War many had fought extremely well, as witnessed by their comparatively heavy casualties, until they were given the order to withdraw. It was a widely believed fallacy that his physical standard was low, as physical fitness had always been emphasized in the Egyptian army, for the men if not always for the officers. While the officers had prestige, the soldiers did not, and the fellaheen, the peasant class, usually far removed from the war, were convinced that the army was nothing to do with them, and unless their sons happened to be drafted into it they tried to ignore it.

After the Khartoum conference the Egyptian army shed its former dual capability, of being ready to march into Israel and at the same time having an expeditionary role, and was forced to adopt a new one—that of the defence of Egypt. Nasser had always favoured having an expeditionary capability, which he had exercised in the Yemen in furtherance of his policies, and he had always been opposed in this by Marshal Amer, who had constantly advised that the Egyptian army should have just one aim, that of marching eastwards to destroy Israel. The position was now drastically changed, and although lip-service was given to developing the capability to advance into the Sinai to attack Israel, in reality, encouraged strongly by the Soviet military mission, all efforts were turned to defence, and the Egyptians likened themselves in the days after the June War to the British after Dunkirk and drew many parallels to bolster their morale and fortitude.

The Soviet policy of having a fleet in the Mediterranean to counter that of America enabled Egypt to have a larger navy than its coastline and resources warranted. For example, the Russians built a large shipyard at Alexandria obviously for repair of ships of the Soviet fleet, and constructed naval facilities at other Egyptian ports, which, of course, also benefited the Egyptian navy. The Egyptian navy gained an unexpected and fortuitous boost when it sank the *Eilat*, and its morale was quite high. Like the Israeli navy it did not have much chance to win glory during the June War, and in fact it had to retreat hurriedly from Port Said to Alexandria to avoid the attention of Israeli aircraft. With a strength of about 12,000 men, the Egyptian navy consisted basically of six destroyers, 21 submarines, 46 MTBs, 32 patrol and escort ships, 21 landing craft and eight mine-sweepers. Its most modern and potent craft were 18 Soviet missile ships, ten of the Osa Class and eight of the Komar Class, both carrying the Styx[1] surface-to-surface missile, the standard armament on Soviet fast patrol ships. The 160-ton Osa Class had two pairs of launchers, and the 100-ton Komar Class had just a single pair, both craft having a speed of 40 knots.

Never very robust, the Egyptian national economy had taken a severe tumble after the June War: the Suez Canal was closed, losing the country some £74 million annually; the small oil wells on the western coast of the lower Sinai peninsula were in Israeli hands; and the lucrative tourist trade had dried up. The cotton crop, the mainstay of the economy for years, was not a good one in 1967, part being infected with leaf worm, and in any event most of it was mortgaged to the Soviet Union for material supplied. In July there was an economy budget, when taxes were raised, workers' compulsory savings were increased to 50 per cent and extra duty was placed on imported luxury goods. The Egyptians, for example, were encouraged to eat macaroni instead of rice, which was exported to raise cash and credit.

The actions of the Soviet Union were at times paradoxical; it reinforced failure by pouring more modern arms into Egypt, and at the same time it supported the closure of the Suez Canal, at least for a while, which meant that its military aid to Vietnam had to be shipped there by way of the Cape of Good Hope to Haiphong, a sea journey of some 14,000 miles instead of only 7,000, as the Chinese Government would not allow Soviet goods to be sent across its territory. For months the Soviet Union showed little interest in a Middle East settlement, and although it did not need the oil in the Middle East, it was anxious to deny it to the Western Powers. Soviet naval presence in the Mediterranean was increased until, by January 1968, there were nearly 50 Soviet ships overshadowing those of the US 6th Fleet.

Israel was a much smaller country than Egypt, both in size and

[1] NATO designation.

population, consisting of some 7,992 square miles before the June War and having about 2·3 million Jews (additionally about 300,000 Arabs lived in Israel). Unlike that of Egypt, the population was geared to war and had been for years; some 264,000 people could be mobilized into the armed forces within 72 hours, of whom some 30 per cent were women. Born into strife and trouble, Israel forcibly emerged as a state in 1948, beating back Arab soldiers; again, in 1956, Israel defeated the Egyptians in the Sinai. Being too small and much too narrow for any form of defence in depth, Israeli defence policy had been to attack and carry the war into any enemy country, which it had done successfully so far. Mobility, speed and an armoured punch had been the basic factors in Israeli military strategy, which was formulated and directed by the youthful but competent, practical and clear-thinking general staff. The June War brought the Israelis an additional 26,000 square miles of territory, together with one million Arabs to administer. Now Israel had much more space in which to manoeuvre, and especially valuable was the Sinai. Also the cease-fire lines were shorter by a few miles, straighter and more defensible than the pre-June War boundaries, the Suez Canal being an example.

The brigade, or regimental combat team, had been retained as the basic field formation, there being some 31 on full mobilization. Of these 22 were infantry (two having a paratroop capability), eight were armoured and one was a paratroop brigade. The 'teeth' element of the Israeli army amounted to about 130,000 men, thus making a ratio of 'teeth' to 'tail' of 50:50, slightly higher than that of the Egyptian army, and much higher than most Western armies, whose ratio was usually much nearer 20:80. Israeli military equipment was miscellaneous and much of it was elderly, having been accumulated as and whenever possible, depending upon the vagaries of the current world political situation. In round figures, before the June War the Israelis possessed about 800 tanks, 250 self-propelled guns and 300 US M-3 half-tracks. Material losses in the June War had been small and had been more than compensated for by pressing into service captured or abandoned Egyptian equipment.

Much of the credit for Israeli success in the June War must go to Major-General Rabin, the Chief of Staff, his predecessors and the general staff, who had forged the Israeli defences forces (IDF) into the splendid instrument they had proved to be. The general staff controlled the air force and the navy as well as the army. The Defence Minister, Moshe Dayan, himself a former Chief-of-Staff, a flamboyant personality, had only come back on to the military scene on the eve of the war, but his leadership and flair for battle had instilled dash and confidence into the Israelis, military and civilian, at just the right moment. The Premier, Levi Eshkol, has been over-shadowed, blamed and generally underrated, as although he lacked decisiveness when it was required in emergency, favouring rather a slow concensus of opinion, he was a shrewd statesman and politician who had done much for Israel, especially when he was Finance Minister.

On the 3rd December General Rabin relinquished his post as Chief-of-Staff at the end of his extended tour of duty, and was appointed Israeli Ambassador to America. His place was taken by Major-General Haim Bar-Lev, the Deputy Chief-of-Staff, and, as he was then aged 43, it meant continuing the principle of a youthful general staff. Born in Austria and educated in Yugoslavia, General Bar-Lev came to Palestine in 1939, and served in the Haganah before becoming a regular in the IDF when it emerged in the 1948 War. He commanded an armoured brigade in the 1956 fighting, and had also been Chief of Operations, which meant that he had been part of the planning team for some years, so there was a continuity of Israeli strategic policy and planning. On the 1st July 1968 Ygal Alon, a former commander of the famous Palmach Brigade in the 1948 War, was appointed Deputy Premier; this was considered significant by both the Russians and the Arabs, as they felt that although the colourful Moshe Dayan was more frequently to the fore and in the news, the quieter, thoughtful Alon was more dangerous to them in the long run.

In Egypt, in February 1968, the verdicts of the military tribunal trying the four senior air force officers were announced. Mohammed Mahmoud Sidky, former commander, was sentenced to 15 years' imprisonment, and Ismail Labib was sentenced to 10 years, while Gamal Afift, former Chief of Air Staff, and Hamid el-Dogeidy, former Commander of the Eastern Zone, were acquitted. Nasser was no longer directly associated in the public mind with military failure and the strong feeling now within Egypt was that the armed forces had let the country down. A few days later, on the 21st, there were demonstrations by factory workers at Helwan, about 15 miles south of Cairo. Next, during the week-end of the 24th/25th February, rioting occurred in Cairo, mainly by students, against the leniency of the military tribunal, and some students took this opportunity to demand a return to parliamentary government, free speech and more private enterprise. There were still many in Egypt who wanted a reorientation of Egyptian policy away from pan-Arabism and towards the Nile Valley. Some 60 police and 20 students were injured, many students were arrested and some universities were closed down. The censored Egyptian press made little mention of these riots.

These demonstrations caused the Government anxiety. After a cabinet meeting on the 26th February, General Fawzi, who had taken over as Defence Minister in January 1968 from Amin Howeidi, decided not to confirm the sentences, but instead ordered a retrial, a decision obviously forced by public opinion. On the 3rd March Nasser addressed a meeting of workers at Helwan, stating that the recent demonstrations were due to a 'series of misunderstandings'. He also said that there was an organized 'counter-revolutionary party' in Egypt waiting for a chance to seize power. Helwan had been established as a model factory complex, and so the demonstrations and unrest there were doubly unsettling for the Government.

On the 20th March President Nasser reorganized his cabinet, dropping several military officers, including Zakharia Moheiddin, who had extreme right-wing views, and Ali Sabry, who held left-wing ones, and bringing in 14 civilians, who included engineers, intellectuals, bankers and professional men. This gave his cabinet more of a 'technocratic' character, and less of a military one.

It was not until the 26th August 1968 that some verdicts of the military tribunal were next announced, and they included five life sentences, many imprisonments and 15 acquittals. Of the four senior air force officers, Sidky and Labib were given increased prison sentences, and again Afift and Dogeidy were acquitted. By this time the heat had gone out of the situation and these announcements caused no public outcry or other reaction.

President Nasser turned his attention to the Arab Socialist Union, the only permitted political party in Egypt, and on the 30th March 1968 he announced that it was to be reformed so that its roots rested on the basis of popular enfranchisement, and that a plebiscite on his proposals would be held in May. Ali Sabry was put in charge of the reorganization, the object of which officially was to concentrate all military, economic and ideological forces against the enemy, and also to mobilize the popular masses, their potentialities and energies. On the 2nd May the plebiscite produced a 99·9 per cent vote in favour, but there was a proviso that the 'grass roots elections' would not be held until the Israelis had been defeated. Egypt remained a one-party state. President Nasser made a show of mustering the Arabs against Israel, and on the 30th April he appointed Lieutenant-General Talat Hassan, an Egyptian general, to be Chief-of-Staff of the Unified Arab High Command, a superstructure designed to mobilize and direct the military efforts of the 110 million Arabs against Israel. The position had been vacant since the June War.

Although there were deliveries of some SAM-2s to Egypt in April by this time the flow of Soviet arms had slowed down almost to a stop, and this caused Nasser to visit the Soviet Union in July, where he had talks with Soviet leaders. He asked for more and heavier arms, as he wanted sufficient to give him material superiority over the Israelis, but the Russians refused, on the score that he had not yet absorbed the arms already sent. Shortly after his return to Egypt Nasser again flew to the Soviet Union, to Georgia, for medical treatment, where he remained for a fortnight. The Soviet leaders had given verbal backing, hesitating to send more arms, but after a while they relented to a degree; in October it was reported that some SAMs had arrived in Egypt, together with controlling technicians, some radar-guided 57mm anti-aircraft guns and some ground-to-ground unguided, spin stabilized tactical missiles of the FROG series.[1]

During the first half of 1968 the whole length of the Suez Canal front, although raw and touchy, was fairly quiet, there being little hostility apart from sporadic shelling, but heavier bombardments in July, September and October led to reprisals. The first artillery duel of any size occurred on the 8th July, in the region of Suez town, the Egyptians alleging that 43 civilians were killed and 70 injured, as well as 150 houses destroyed. The Israelis claimed that the

[1] These were probably the FROG (Free Rocket Over Ground)-3s (NATO code name) which had been in Soviet service since 1960–61. Fitted with a cylindrical bulbous warhead, and mounted on a PT76 tracked vehicle, the missiles had a range of about 30 miles, the vehicle acting as the launcher. Known to the Russians as the Lunik series.

Egyptians opened fire first, and that they had been forced to reply to it, but this was denied by the Egyptians.

The next heavy artillery exchange was on the 8th September. Lasting for about four hours, it extended along much of the length of the southern part of the Canal, shells often being fired at point-blank range into positions on the opposite bank. It had begun after the ambush of an Israeli patrol by Egyptian commandos, and it was estimated (by the Israelis) that some 12,000 shells were fired along a 70-mile front by both sides. This time the Egyptians claimed that they lost ten killed, five soldiers and five civilians, and that 30 were injured, while considerable damage had been done to houses and harbour installations at Port Suez and Port Tewfik. They said that they had inflicted damage on Israeli positions and equipment, claiming to have knocked out 14 tanks and six armoured vehicles. The Israelis admitted to ten killed and 18 wounded. On the 10th, in another heavy barrage, the Egyptians were estimated (by the Israelis) to have pumped another 10,000 shells into Israeli positions along the east bank. The Israelis were alarmed at the amount of ammunition being expended in case it were a preliminary to an assault crossing in force, so they called up more reservists and moved another brigade forward to the area of Mitla.

During the summer Egyptian commandos tentatively tried out a few crossings of the Canal, mostly at night and in small groups, mainly with the object of laying mines and then quickly returning to their own side of the waterway, in the manner of the Fedayeen, who were operating similar tactics into Israel from Jordan at the time amid great acclaim. Later they tried small ambushes, claiming some success, but it was difficult to gauge exactly how much; the Israelis were silent on this aspect for several weeks, as they did not want to upset the morale of their own forward troops. However, on the 26th August they did admit to an ambush incident on their side of the Canal about three miles south of the Great Bitter Lakes, in which Egyptian commandos ambushed one of their jeeps, killing two soldiers and 'kidnapping' another.

The next artillery barrages across the Canal, the heaviest ever, began on the late afternoon of the 26th October, spreading like wildfire between Kantara and Port Suez, and on this occasion Katyusha rockets were brought into action as well. The Israelis were almost caught off-guard, some soldiers being killed while playing football just behind their positions. The Israelis, who stopped firing first, lost 15 killed and had 34 wounded, their largest casualty toll since the sinking of the *Eilat*. The Egyptians reported 12 killed, and many houses destroyed and damaged, but claimed that Israeli losses included '19 tanks, 14 half-tracks, 10 missile sites, 28 machine-gun positions, 16 observation posts, three command posts, six fuel and ammunition dumps and three 106mm guns'. Three oil storage tanks were set on fire at Suez, where one of the two refineries burnt out the previous October (1967) had been rebuilt by the Russians. Until this moment the Israelis had not shelled it for fear of inflicting Soviet casualties. A later UN report (of the 28th October) stated that the Egyptians had initiated the attack, and had three times refused to comply with UN requests to stop firing.

Under cover of this firing, which lasted several hours, a small party of Egyptians crossed the Canal near Ishmailia, and penetrated some distance along the road to Mitla, where at about midnight they ambushed two Israeli jeeps, wounding one soldier, before withdrawing to recross the Canal just before dawn. The Egyptians were elated and referred to this as the Mitla Pass operation, feeling that they were now both capable of mounting tremendous artillery barrages and, more important, that they could also recross the Canal, an offensive gesture that made them feel good and gave their morale a lift.

The Israelis had come off second best; out-gunned, the density of the shelling had caught them by surprise and had shaken them. The Israeli general staff estimated that the Egyptians had deployed about 600 guns and some rockets for this operation. The Israelis had deployed only two infantry brigades, totalling some 10,000 who were strung out along a 110-mile front[1] in small defensive posts at intervals along the bank, surveillance being kept by patrols, on foot and in vehicles, between them, while relying upon small mobile groups, from the two armoured brigades lying back some 20–30 miles in the low ridge of hills, to repel hostile landings. When counter-battery fire was required, Israeli guns, which were mainly self-propelled 155mm howitzers, mounted on US M-4 Sherman chassis, and AMX tanks fitted with the 105 howitzer, were rushed

[1] The Suez Canal was actually 99 miles in length. The extra mileage includes the 'turning' eastward of the defences at the northern end, and an extension at the southern end.

forward to the Canal, where they constantly changed positions after firing and then, when it was over, were sent back several miles to wait under cover for their next task.

The Israeli answer, on the night of the 30th October, was a raid deep into Egypt with troops transported by helicopters to disrupt installations at, and near, Nag Hamadi (population about 20,000) on the River Nile about 140 miles inland from the Red Sea, where they blew up a transformer and switching station controlling the high tension power cables between Cairo and Aswan. Other targets were the Nile Bridge at Nag Hamadi, the Nile bridge at nearby Qena (population about 40,000) and the adjacent irrigation sluice gates, all of which were partly demolished. Qena was at a road junction between routes from the Red Sea area and routes that ran north to south in the Nile Valley. The Israelis announced that all their forces returned safely, published pictures of the damage caused, and stated that the object of the raid was to 'demonstrate the power of Israeli forces to reply to, and deter, Egyptian aggression'. The Israelis afterwards admitted that naval craft, helicopters and jeeps had been used in this operation.

The Israelis were known to have at least three French Super Frelon helicopters, the Sud 321, able to carry about 30 fully equipped soldiers for a radius of about 300 miles, and a few Sikorski UH-34s,[1] which could carry up to 18 fully equipped troops for a radius of 140 miles. The Super Frelons were used for the raid, each carrying a group of Israeli commandos detailed to deal separately with each of the objectives.

Shocked by this deep penetration raid, the Egyptian general staff refused to admit that Israeli troops had landed so far inside Egypt, insisting that the damage had been done by aerial bombing and rocket fire. There was also disquiet as the targets had been on the main north-south line of communication between Cairo and Aswan, some 560 miles apart along the Nile Valley. The Aswan Dam, upon which so much depended, and then 96 per cent completed, was frequently referred to by Egyptians as 'our future'. When completed it was expected to increase fertile land in the Upper Nile Valley by 1·5 million acres, and to allow double-cropping in another 4 million acres. On the 3rd November it was announced that a popular defence army, on the lines of Britain's wartime Home Guard, was to be

[1] Known in Britain as the Wessex.

formed in Egypt to protect key installations and utilities. After the Nag Hamadi raid Egyptian pressure on the Suez Canal Front slackened and it was five months before another really heavy artillery barrage took place.

Despite their usually efficient intelligence service, the Israeli general staff and the Government had been shocked too, as it had become suddenly obvious that the Egyptians had received and massed along the Canal many more guns, some of heavy calibre, than had been realized, so the Israelis energetically set to work to 'harden' their forward Canal defences. The Nag Hamadi raid had shown the long reach of the Israelis and caused the Egyptian general staff to be less abrasive. Had it instead taken a bolder course and continued to pound the largely unprotected Israelis on the east bank with heavy and continuous artillery barrages, they most probably would have forced them to withdraw back out of range. Had this occurred there would have been a 20-mile wide belt of territory along the eastern side of the Canal in which it would have been hazardous for Israeli troops to remain in any number for long, and so make Egyptian commando or assault landings much easier. The Egyptians failed to exploit a tactical advantage and so missed one of their greatest tactical opportunities in this war across the Suez Canal when it was in its early stages.

By this time the Soviet Union had replaced about 80 per cent of Egyptian material losses of the June War, and as new weapons were distributed and units reformed and trained a new spirit of confidence, developing into aggressiveness, slowly surged through the army. While it was tacitly admitted that the Egyptians would not be ready to face the Israelis on the battlefield until 1970, two years hence, the army, which only 16 months previously had suffered a disastrous defeat, had come up to challenge the Israeli army shot for shot, and come off best, which gave it cause for renewed pride.

All this fighting across the Suez Canal should be seen against a larger Middle East background. Elsewhere, nourished by Syria, the cult of the Fedayeen was rising again[1] as Palestinian guerillas became active. Their first attempt to infiltrate into the west bank, now occupied by the Israelis, to practise the dictum of Mao Tse-tung of the guerilla fighter 'fish' swimming in the 'sea' of the one million Arabs under Israeli administration, failed and the Israelis had rooted

[1] See *Arab Guerilla Power* by Edgar O'Ballance.

most of the Palestinian guerillas out by the end of 1967. This largely compelled the Fedayeen to undertake commando and infiltration raids into Israel from Jordan, which provoked Israeli retaliation. One large reprisal raid on Karameh, a Jordanian village near the Israeli cease-fire line, where some 3,000 guerillas mostly in training, were based in March 1968, had only been partially successful, and while it forced the guerillas to withdraw a few miles back from Israeli reach to avoid such attention, it was turned into a Fedayeen victory by guerilla propaganda.

During the remainder of 1968 enthusiasm for the mystique of the Fedayeen swept throughout the Arab world. By the end of that year Fatah, the largest guerilla organization, was reputed to have a strength of over 20,000 guerillas, while money and arms poured in from many sources. It was a period of rapid expansion in which Fedayeen organizations multiplied until there were as many as 20 or so, all independent of each other. Many had conflicting aims and ideologies, but all were ostensibly dedicated to bringing about the downfall of Israel.

The Israeli frontier with the Lebanon was quiet, as was that with Syria, that country refusing, to avoid reprisals, to allow itself to become a springboard for guerilla operations into Israel, but in Jordan, where the guerillas were taking full advantage of the weak military and political situation, the border with Israel was very much alive. Soon, in Jordan, guerillas were jostling King Hussein's soldiers on the streets of Amman, openly walking about armed and in uniform. The Fedayeen sought to be independent of all national restraints, demanding freedom of movement and assistance. After clashes with the Jordanian security forces, Arab public opinion was so much in favour of the guerillas and their professed ideals that King Hussein was forced to come to the 'November Agreement' with them—really a 'live-and-let-live arrangement', neither giving away any more than compelled to—instead of using military force to bring them to heel. In Egypt President Nasser sought to collect in and dominate the diverse Fedayeen leadership and to make Cairo the centre and headquarters of guerilla manipulation, but he would not allow the guerilla fighters to operate from Egyptian soil or give them any of the freedoms they were trying to snatch in other Arab countries.

3 · The Quest for Arms

'War (is) the only remaining possibility'
MOHAMMED HASSENEIN HEIKAL,
Editor of *Al Ahram*

After the Nag Hamadi raid in October 1968 friction along the line of the Suez Canal died down for several weeks, enabling both Egypt and Israel to continue with military preparations and to attempt to obtain more arms. But both countries also had internal political problems to overcome. In Egypt, on the 21st November, student riots flared up at Mansoura in the Delta, started by high-school boys, who were soon joined by university students. Police had to turn out in force and by the end of the day four people had been killed and over 40 injured. The demonstrators demanded educational reforms, the abolition of secret police and censorship, and more parliamentary democracy. Reaction quickly spread to Alexandria University, where police were called to deal with students staging a 'sit-in' and other demonstrations. On the 24th all universities[1] in Egypt and the 14 higher educational establishments were closed until further notice. On the 25th rioting at the Alexandria University spilled out on to the streets, where students were joined by workers, and before it subsided 16 people had been killed and over 100 injured.

On the following day, the 26th, Egyptian aircraft and helicopters swooped low over Cairo in a show of force to impress would-be rioters, and censorship was imposed on press reports sent out of the country. Mahmoud Riad,[2] the Foreign Minister, in an interview said that the riots at Mansoura and Alexandria were part of a world disease that had not affected other parts of Egypt, while Editor Heikal in *Al Ahram* warned the Egyptians not to take them too

---

[1] There are five universities—Cairo, Alexandria, Ain Shams, Asyut and the Al-Azhar.
[2] Not to be confused with Abdul Munein Riad, Chief of Staff of the Armed Forces.

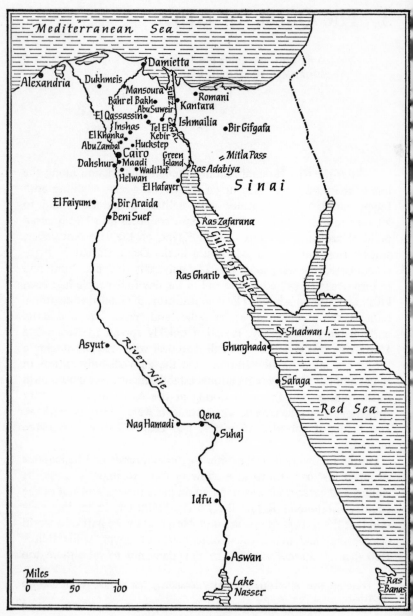

Egypt and the Suez Canal Zone

lightly. The central committee of the ASU met twice to consider their implications.

On the 2nd December President Nasser addressed a specially convened session of the congress of the ASU at which he expressed surprise at the actions of the students and blamed opportunists, non-nationalist elements and an 'Israeli agent' who infiltrated student bodies. Two days later he told the same congress that a political settlement was one in which 'Israel will not stay on a single inch of the lands of any Arab country'. On the 8th he said that Egypt might be prepared to accept another UN force in connexion with a general Middle East settlement.

The Egyptians were not too worried about the Russian attitude, but they speculated uneasily on that of America in regard to the Middle East. The conclusion, as outlined in one of Editor Heikal's weekly articles, which were generally thought to reflect Nasser's private views, was that American political influence in the Middle East had dwindled altogether and the growing Soviet presence was out-flanking NATO at a time when the West, owing to the summer Soviet invasion of Czechoslovakia, was fully aware of its weakness. Concluding that a political settlement with Israel was impossible, and that the rebuilding of the Egyptian armed forces should have 'incomparable priority', he wrote that 'In March 1968 a military showdown with the Israelis over the liberation of the occupied territories was one of several alternatives; by September 1968 it was the only remaining possibility'. Nasser was then convinced that combined Soviet and Arab pressure had persuaded America to reconsider its aid programme to Israel, a view which had been encouraged by President Johnson's refusal to supply that country with Phantom aircraft.

In October elections at higher committee level were held in the ASU, as being the next stage in Nasser's political reorganization of the Union, in which Anwar Sadat was elected political secretary only, while Ali Sabry was merely elected secretary of an organizing sub-committee. Although Sadat, and indeed Sabry, were Nasser faithfuls, this was not quite what Nasser wanted, so he stepped in and postponed further executive elections, which left the power still in Ali Sabry's hands. However, Sabry suffered a heart attack shortly afterwards and was compelled to fade away from the political scene for a while.

On the 8th January 1969 the Egyptians went to the polls to elect a new National Assembly, this being the final stage of Nasser's promised political reforms. On the 20th he addressed the new members, saying that a political solution to the Arab-Israeli conflict was impossible until the enemy realized that the Arabs could force him to withdraw by fighting. Nasser believed that any Arab leader at this stage who attempted to make peace with the Israelis would inevitably meet the same fate as King Abdullah of Jordan, who had been assassinated in 1951 reputedly for trying to come to an agreement with Israel. By holding this rigid attitude he was able to convince the Egyptian people that the Israelis had no intention of leaving the occupied territories. Touching on the 'home front', Nasser told the new National Assembly that industry and agriculture continued to improve, emphasized the benefits the Aswan Dam would bring, and said that the oil industry in Egypt was to be developed. An American company had leased an off-shore oilfield in the Gulf of Suez, which had estimated reserves of one billion barrels, while another foreign company was already pumping some 40,000 barrels a day from wells near El Alamein. It was anticipated that Egyptian oil production would rise to about 450,000 barrels a day by 1970.

On the 8th October the Israelis put their peace plan to the UN, but the Arabs shyed away from it, mainly because of its omissions rather than its content, and also because the Israelis did not specify their future intentions. The next day Foreign Minister Riad formally rejected it, and once again demanded that first the Israelis withdraw from the occupied territories; but on the 14th November Moshe Dayan commented that the Israelis were prepared to pay a high price for peace that might include the return of the occupied territories, which made the Arabs think that if they stood firm the Israelis might eventually back down. Following complaints by one side or the other, there had been several debates in the UN during 1968, but nothing was resolved, and Gunnar Jarring had shuttled fruitlessly from one capital to the other.

Meanwhile, Fedayeen activity began to rock the Middle East. On the 26th December 1968 two Palestinian guerillas attacked an El Al airliner at Athens airport, killing one passenger and injuring an air hostess; the guerillas claimed that El Al had ferried home Israeli pilots who had been training on Phantom aircraft in America. On the

28th December Israeli commandos in helicopters raided Beirut airport, destroying 12 Arab airliners on the ground in 45 minutes and causing damage to the estimated amount of £40 million; the reason given was that Palestinian guerillas had their headquarters in the Lebanon and also trained there.

So far Nasser had always given verbal support to the Fedayeen, although firmly restricting their activities in Egypt, and Cairo remained the meeting place for the Palestine Liberation Organization, which sponsored the Palestine Liberation Army, of which some 4,000 men were in Egypt in the Canal Zone. On the 4th February 1969 Yassir Arafat, the prominent guerilla personality, became chairman of the PLO, while remaining head of Fatah, after which he was frequently in contact with Nasser, each leader hoping to influence the other.

On the 10th February Arafat was quick off the mark, announcing the transfer of the PLA brigade in Egypt to Jordan. This project presumably had been agreed to by Nasser, but King Hussein of Jordan had not been consulted, and Arab opinion was suspicious. King Hussein certainly did not want any more guerillas in his country at the time, as he had already more than he was able to deal with. A few days later the idea was dropped, the original report denied, and the PLA brigade stayed in Egypt.[1]

Israel had been governed by coalitions since its inception as a state. As it had proportional representation there was a multiplicity of political parties each with a varying number of representatives in the Knesset. In the past there had been many attempts at mergers with the aim of one party being able to gain a workable majority. On the 20th January 1969 a covenant of alliance between the Israeli Labour Party and the left-wing Mapam (United Workers' Party) came into being, and this new merger gave the ILP 62 of the 120 seats in the Knesset. The ILP itself had come into being the previous year (on the 21st January 1968) as the result of the merger of the Mapai, Ahdut Avoda and Rafi Parties. On the 12th February a motion of 'no confidence' in Premier Eshkol was defeated in the Knesset, following controversy over an interview given by him to a journalist in which he stated that Israel was not interested in

---

[1] Nasser was not able to get rid of any of the PLA brigade until August 1970, just after his cease-fire with Israel, when during the Jordanian civil war he dispatched 3,000 of them into Syria.

any of the populated areas of the west bank, but only in a small military presence along the River Jordan, at Jerusalem and at Sharm El Sheikh.[1] There was a very strong trend in Israel that favoured holding on to, and settling, large parts of the occupied territories.

On the 26th February Premier Eshkol died of a heart attack, and Ygal Alon, the Deputy Premier, headed the Government temporarily, until the central committee of the ILP chose Mrs Golda Meir to succeed him, on the 7th March. One of the founders of the Mapai Party, now 71 years of age, she had been born in Russia and taken to America as a young girl, where she became a school teacher, before emigrating to Palestine in 1921. During the days of the Mandate she was politically active in the Jewish Agency, and just before the outbreak of the first Arab-Israeli War in 1948, disguised as an Arab woman, she went through hostile territory to have talks with King Abdullah of Trans-Jordan. She had been the first Israeli Ambassador to the Soviet Union after that war, and then held other key posts, including that of Foreign Minister. There was some speculation whether Moshe Dayan, of the Rafi Party, would serve in her cabinet, if asked, or oppose her and perhaps persuade his party to leave the political alliance, but he agreed to remain in the cabinet as Minister of Defence, which meant continuity in defence policies. On the 19th March Premier Meir emphasized Israeli unwillingness to have any UN force on Israeli soil.

One of the main Israeli anxieties was to know exactly what the Russians wanted in the Middle East, and how far they were prepared to go to get it. Also, there was an acute distrust of Nasser by the Israeli leadership. Accordingly, Israel had to remain in a high state of military preparedness, and this burden lay heavily on the country, absorbing some 20 per cent of the gross national product and some 25 per cent of its industrial output. Taxation on the individual was heavy too, and additionally a sum of money was taken from salaries and wage packets for defence, but there were few grumbles, as most appreciated the necessity for this.

Limited by international political restraints and by financial restrictions, Israel had continual difficulty in obtaining the amount and type of arms it estimated it required to defend itself adequately. For some years it had been struggling to establish a home arms

[1] Renamed Ophis by the Israelis.

industry. This had been hampered by lack of material, help and encouragement from the major powers, as they suspected that it might upset their own individual idea of the correct military balance in the Middle East, but despite this the Israelis managed to produce many military items that included small arms, mortars, ammunition, spares and personal equipment, as well as assembling trucks and jeeps. The Uzi sub-machine carbine, completely designed and produced by the Israelis, had been in service with the IDF for some years and had been bought in small quantities by other armies. The French embargo on arms in the June War made the Israelis fear that their one source of sophisticated weapons might dry up, and so they renewed their efforts to develop their home arms industries.

The first progress report, in January 1969,[1] stated that over 20 factories employing over 5,000 people were producing material to the value of £42 million annually, which included ammunition for all the guns and jet cannon possessed, electronic and communications equipment, and a wide range of spare parts for weapons and vehicles. A fast tank of advanced design, with a 300-mile radius of action, known as the Shoot Kol, based on the American M-48, with a diesel engine and mounting a 105mm gun, was being developed, as was a television-guided, air-to-ground missile, a 90mm anti-tank gun mounted on a half-track vehicle (the old American M-3) and a new rifle, while the Israeli surface-to-surface missile, the Gabriel, was in service with the Israeli navy. Israel was also becoming quite advanced in the computer field, already there being over 100 in use in the country, with more on order. Few additional details have since been released, but taking into consideration later American technical assistance, the Israeli arms industrial base must have expanded considerably.

Back in Egypt the Soviet Union was anxious to find some means of both controlling the large quantities of arms it was sending to Egypt, and of ensuring that the guns were pointing the correct way— that is, against Western imperialism. Early in October 1968 Marshal Yakubovsky, the Soviet Chief of Staff, visited Egypt and inspected positions in the Suez Canal Zone, and he made his report to a meeting of defence ministers of the Warsaw Pact countries in Moscow on the 29th October. Marshal Yakubovsky was back in

[1] *Jerusalem Post* of the 18th January 1969.

Egypt on the 2nd November, this time to watch military exercises. On the 5th the Soviet Union proposed a form of Arab joint association between Egypt, Syria and Iraq, all countries to which the Soviet Union was currently sending arms, and the Warsaw Pact organization, but this was doubtfully received by the Arabs.[1] On the 21st the Soviet Foreign Minister arrived in Cairo for a three-day stay to have talks with President Nasser and Foreign Minister Riad.

President Johnson, of the USA, had tended to let both sides work out their own differences amongst themselves, and he had withdrawn himself as much as he could from Middle East problems, which had allowed the Soviet Union to appear to have a free hand in the Arab countries. When the Nixon administration came into office in January 1969, it adopted a different attitude, and instigated a series of talks that encouraged a revival of Four Power interest. Later, on the 26th March, when Hafez al-Assad, the Syrian head of state, called for a federal union between Syria, Egypt and Iraq, there was no mention or thought of any contact or alliance with the Warsaw Pact defence organization—the Soviet idea had not taken root.

On the 16th November 1968 the Egyptian Government set up a National Defence Council, with President Nasser as chairman, to prepare the country for war. Later, on the day following the heavy Israeli raids on Fedayeen camps in Syria on the 24th February (1969), a state of emergency was proclaimed in Egypt, which meant a 'maximum alert' for the Popular Defence Army, the police and the civil defence elements, including fire brigades, hospital and certain municipal services. It seemed to the Israelis that war clouds were fast gathering and they felt that the Egyptians might be ready to launch a major attack against them in the autumn of 1969. Accordingly, they reconsidered their strategy and tactics. They had found, for example, in the June War how costly it was in casualties frontally to assault fixed defensive positions of the Soviet pattern, and the emphasis veered towards commando raiding and flank activities, rather than infantry set-piece attacks backed by conventional supporting weapons. With this in mind a new post was created in the IDF, that of Director of Paratroops and Infantry, to which was appointed Brigadier Rafoul, who had been wounded when leading

[1] The *New Middle East* of December 1968.

a unit of paratroops in the northern part of the Sinai during the June War. His brief was to train the infantry, and especially the paratroops, in commando raiding tactics.

By the end of 1968 there were still feelings of discontent in Egypt and disillusionment among sections of the people. As Nasser sat in the seat of political power as secretary-general of the ASU, he must have felt it listing from side to side, being pulled by the Left, which felt that socialism had not been taken far enough, and then by the Right which thought it had gone too far. But both extremes preferred to see Nasser, who still remained head and shoulders above the minority of confused and disunited groupings, in power as the lesser evil, rather than any of their opponents.

Egypt as a country had become dull rather than war-weary, and Cairo seemed to be a drab city where luxury goods had been banned mainly to save foreign exchange, and where for many months most people had three 'meatless days' a week. Previously the middle and educated classes, being inward looking, had tended to blame Nasser for involvement in the war in the Yemen, and it was not until the June defeat that they came to agree that Israel was the real enemy, and that Nasser might be right in his attitude. About 10,000 professional people emigrated annually, but the Government was not unduly worried as it meant jobs becoming available for students as they graduated. To the Fellaheen, the peasant who worked in the fields, and who formed the majority of the population, the threat of Israel continued to be remote and unreal; the war meant little to the man who had to work just as long and just as hard as ever before.

President Nasser, generally known to the man-in-the-street as the 'Rais', or boss, was in the predicament that he must always talk about war, and try to show that he was about to take action against the Israelis, in order to gain and retain the confidence of his people, his armed forces, the ASU, other Arab states and the Fedayeen. Frequently he declared in public that he would not go down in history as the Arab leader who made peace with Israel. He had assumed personal responsibility and command since the June War. He doubted whether he could survive another defeat politically, and although he dared not say so, he was in no hurry to commence hostilities. He described his strategy against Israel as being in three phases, that of Samud, which meant standing fast and not admitting defeat, that of

Radda, or retaliation, and that of Tahrir, meaning victory and the liberation of the occupied lands.

By the beginning of 1969 the entire command structure of the armed forces had been reorganized on Soviet lines, and the combatant element of the army grouped into three 'armies'—the Soviet 'army' being somewhat the equivalent to the Western corps. Two of these, each of about 50,000 men, designated the 6th army and the 7th army, each consisting basically of two infantry and one armoured division, were in positions in the Canal Zone. One, based on the high ground between Cairo and the Delta, covered the area northwards from Ishmailia, with infantry units well forward and armoured ones lying back a few miles. The other 'army' was in a similar disposition to the south of Ishmailia down to and including the Port Suez area, the Zone co-ordinating headquarters being at Ishmailia. The third army (undesignated), still in the process of formation, was to the south of Cairo inland.[1]

The new Soviet equipment was being steadily absorbed, with instructions this time in English, a language practically all Egyptian officers understood, and soon many younger ones were grudgingly admitting that Soviet instructors were good teachers, although hard taskmasters. As more Egyptians learned to use their new weapons, the number of Soviet military personnel in Egypt fell to below the 2,000 mark, and the supply of modern Soviet arms came almost to a stop. The Russians were still prepared to send older models, such as the T-34 tank and other equipment that had become obsolescent in the Soviet army, as it was re-equipped with the more modern, but the Egyptians no longer wanted this old material. They wanted to standardize with modern weapons only, and in fact, in furtherance of this policy they had sent their few remaining British Centurion tanks to Jordan. There was a severe shortage of spares for everything while ammunition, except for the artillery positioned near the Canal, was also in limited supply. The Egyptians, for example, were particularly short of jeep-type vehicles and were trying to buy them through commercial sources by proxy in other Arab countries. It seemed as though the Russians were deliberately keeping the Egyptian armed forces on a tight rein, and they were certainly in no fit state to fight for more than two or three days, except defensively, which must have given Nasser some secret satisfaction

[1] Much later they were re-designated the 1st, 2nd and 3rd Armies.

and allowed him safely to continue his sabre-rattling for political purposes.

Young Egyptian conscripts were taking to the tougher Soviet training and their confidence and morale were rising, as were those of many younger officers who were anxious to prove their worth. A number of Egyptian units were almost fit for battle, or felt they were, but the more realistic counsels of General Riad and the general staff, supported by the Soviet military mission, prevailed, and accordingly Nasser had no opposition to his secret policy. The army generally, and especially the younger officers, were jealous of the reputation being acquired by the Fedayeen, and wanted to eclipse them. Many officers would have liked to occupy the small triangle of territory on the east bank of the Canal at its northern end, where the Egyptians held in token only this small area of swamp and salt marsh by frequent commando patrols, but this would have required a screen of defensive troops well forward past the swamp into the sandy foothills of the Sinai proper, who would be wide open to Israeli armoured attacks. Again, the general staff would not contemplate recommending such an operation to Nasser, being hesitant mainly because the Soviet Union had not committed itself to military action in support of the Egyptians in the event of hostilities. Generally, the Soviet military mission and the Soviet advisers, which were down to units, remained aloof from the Egyptians and unconfiding.

The appearance of an Algerian brigade, which was sent to the central sector of the Canal near Fayid, heartened the Egyptians, who hoped this example would encourage other Arab states to send detachments too, but they were slow to follow suit, the only other Arab force being a unit of Libyans. All along the length of the Canal on the Egyptian side there was an air of stark reality of war as the towns and villages, from which the population had been evacuated, stood empty and deserted, with many buildings demolished or badly damaged. Later, on the 14th February 1969, it was reported that Egypt was ready to allow a survey of the southern part of the Canal to see if it were possible to move out the ships stranded in the Great Bitter Lakes. This was to be undertaken at the owners' expense. The Israelis stated that they would have no objection, provided they first approved of details, but nothing came of this.

Traces of discontent remained in the armed forces, both among the older and senior officers, who still smarted under their treatment after the June War, as well as among the younger officers who were restless at the Government's hesitation to launch them into battle. Some of the younger officers, muttering in secret to each other, could not but remember that Nasser himself rose to power through the army and its discontent. However, the main cause of resentment was the friction between the Egyptian officers and the Soviet advisers, which rose to such a pitch that Nasser visited the Canal Zone on the 27th February to see for himself what the exact situation and feeling were. He was received in many places with an unaccustomed degree of coolness, while younger officers visibly showed signs of impatience, and at times almost asked point-blank when they were going to fight the Israelis.

4 · The War of Attrition

'Israel will hit back with seven blows for every one received'
Premier GOLDA MEIR

Partly to quieten the discontent of the younger officers at the continued inactivity, and partly to demonstrate to the Egyptians, the Arabs and the world at large that he was carrying the war against Israel, on returning from his visit to front-line troops in February 1969 President Nasser, to raise morale, gave authority for artillery barrages to be fired across the Canal at the Israelis on the opposite bank. His artillery regiments had been increased in number to 14, and two more were forming, of which about two-thirds were right forward along the Canal, having between 600 and 700 field guns and mortars. Nasser knew that he out-gunned the Israelis, who held only a thin line of observation posts, that could hardly be called defences, on the east bank, manned by just two infantry brigades strung out, with a back-up armoured brigade in the rear with up to 450 mobile guns in support.

The Canal Zone had been comparatively quiet since the very heavy artillery barrages of the 26th October, since when the Israelis had 'hardened' their paper-thin linear defences into what became known as the Bar-Lev Line, named after General Bar-Lev, the Israeli Chief of Staff. It consisted of a series of multi-storey bunkers, roofed with a 'special material', a combination of rails from the Sinai railway, timber, concrete and sand, able to withstand a direct hit from the 130mm gun, the largest the Egyptians possessed. This claim was largely substantiated and was the reason Israeli casualties were so light throughout the many heavy barrages of 1969.

The smell of war was in the air on both sides, and on the 4th March 1969 Moshe Dayan uttered a warning of the seriousness of the mine-laying and sniping along the length of the Canal by the Egyptians. Two days later, on the 6th, the Egyptians unleashed a heavy artillery barrage across the waterway on to the Bar-Lev Line,

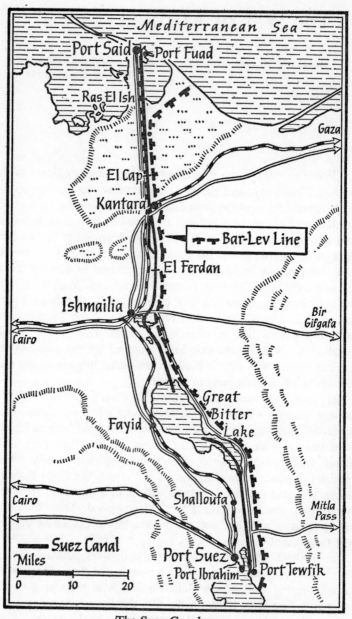

The Suez Canal area

only completed two weeks before, between Kantara and Suez, which continued for five hours before UN observers could bring about a cease-fire. It signalled the opening salvoes of barrages that were to continue at intervals throughout the remainder of the year. The UN later stated (on the 8th) that it had been begun by the Egyptians. After a day of comparative calm, on the 8th another artillery cross-Canal barrage erupted in which hundreds of guns and mortars took part, and it was again later confirmed by the UN that it had been started by the Egyptians. The Israelis replied in kind, and this time fired at the oil refinery at Suez, setting oil storage tanks on fire, the coiled black smoke being visible for miles.

Another artillery battle commenced in the early hours of the 9th, in which an Israeli shell killed General Riad, Chief of Staff of the Armed Forces, who was visiting a forward observation post near Ishmailia. The following day he was accorded a state funeral in Cairo, and was succeeded in his post on the 13th by Lieutenant-General Ahmed Ismail Ali. In this particular exchange of fire the Egyptians claimed to have destroyed five Israeli artillery and mortar batteries, silenced 26, and shot down three Israeli planes, but they admitted damage to the oil refinery, and the loss of four soldiers killed and 39 wounded, together with 72 civilian casualties. In fact, extensive damage had been done to 14 oil storage tanks. The Israelis on their part admitted five killed and 26 wounded, as well as two vehicles destroyed and a Piper Cub aircraft brought down by a SAM-2 missile. The Bar-Lev Line had stood up well to the weight of the barrage.

On the 9th a nation-wide 'black out' was decreed in Egypt, the first since the June War, but it was only slowly and partially implemented, first extending from dousing the huge neon signs in the city to house windows, and then to vehicle headlights which were masked. Technically such 'black outs' were obsolete in an age of electronic detection instruments, such as Israeli aircraft carried, but it brought the war home to the man-in-the-street. The Nile bridges, entrances to Government buildings, post offices and railway stations were protected by sandbags, while anti-blast walls were built in many places. Cairo was seen to be seriously preparing for war, and while no obvious belligerent enthusiasm was evident, as had been the case immediately before the June War, most people seemed resigned to a 'fourth round'.

Egyptian guns were mostly silent on the 10th, the day of General Riad's funeral, but on the following day they all opened up again, just as the Israelis were completing evacuating the last inhabitants from the Arab town of Kantara back to El Arish. A foreign ship in Suez harbour was damaged in the shelling. On the 12th and the 13th, in other artillery battles, storage tanks at the Suez oil refinery were again set on fire. During the remainder of March shell and mortar fire criss-crossed the Canal as an almost daily occurrence, and indeed through April too; the major barrages were on the 18th and 24th March, and on the 4th, 8th, 11th, 13th, 14th and from the 16th to the 20th April. In most cases UN observers managed to bring about a cease-fire within a few hours, and each side invariably accused the other of commencing firing, but the UN later reported that it was usually the Egyptians. In March the Israelis warned that if Egyptian shelling continued they had no intention of sitting forever in their bunkers and that although many obvious reprisal targets were out of range of their guns they were well within reach of their aircraft. On the 8th April the Egyptians began evacuating Port Said, the last place of any size along the Egyptian side of the Canal where any number of civilians remained.

President Nasser now launched his war of attrition in which he meant to grind the Israelis slowly to pieces. He explained to the second congress of the ASU on the 27th March that the Egyptian forces were preparing 'to launch the battle for liberation' against the Israelis. He obviously felt that he was well into his Radda, or retaliation phase, and he warned Israel that the time would come when Egypt would hit Israeli civilian centres in response to attacks by Israelis on towns along the Suez Canal. He also reiterated to the ASU that peace could not be imposed on the area from outside, and that Arabs would not give up the Khartoum conference principles upon which they had stood for two years. He repeated much of what he said in another speech on the 1st April. Some authorities consider that his war of attrition phase commenced on that date, as he also declared the cease-fire agreement of the 9th June 1967 to be null and void.

On the 9th April U Thant announced that Gunnar Jarring, his special representative in the Middle East, had resumed his duties as Swedish Ambassador to the Soviet Union, but would be immediately available whenever developments required his services again. In the meanwhile a series of Big Four talks was taking place. On the 10th April King Hussein of Jordan visited America, and while there addressed the National Press Club in Washington, putting forward a six-point peace plan with which he associated President Nasser's name. The main proposals were that the Arabs should recognize Israel and allow Israeli shipping in the Suez Canal and the Straits of Tiran, in return for their withdrawal from the occupied territories. This was not well received by the Israelis, who still demanded direct negotiation, and there were doubts as to exactly how much Nasser had been consulted on this matter by King Hussein. On the 22nd April U Thant said that a virtual state of war existed along the Suez Canal, that UN efforts had been almost totally ineffective, that there had been major breaches of the cease-fire on each of the last twelve successive days, sometimes extending along the whole length of the waterway, and that weapons used included heavy artillery, heavy mortars, tanks and rockets. Some 586 incidents along the Canal were recorded during April.

Egypt now had 18 well trained, tough commando units, as well as two brigades of paratroops, all selected volunteers, who were anxious to prove their mettle. As much to raise their morale, and that of the younger officers panting for action, Nasser—in addition to shelling during April—authorized a stepping up of commando raids across the canal. On the 19th Egyptian commandos crossed the waterway under the cover of a heavy barrage to attack Israeli positions on the eastern shore of Lake Timsah, claiming to have caused 30 Israeli casualties, but the Israelis said that the raiding party consisted of only 15 Egyptians, who were driven back after a brief gun battle, and that only one Israeli was wounded. During the following night, the 20th, there was another Egyptian commando raid across the Canal, about 20 miles north of Kantara, when both sides made conflicting claims. On the 22nd, in an Egyptian raid, three Israeli soldiers were killed and another captured during the hours of darkness. After this Egyptian commando raids occurred practically every night, and on some nights there were more than one. There was some elation as this safety valve released some of the military tensions, but there was also some apprehension in case the Israelis mounted reprisal attacks, perhaps on Port Said. Editor Heikal, in *Al Ahram*, warned on the 26th that the Egyptians should be ready for heavy losses from Israeli counter-action.

Many Egyptian officers still felt that not enough was being done, and that artillery and mortar barrages, while impressive, were not achieving any positive results, and that although exploited dramatically in propaganda, the commando raids were but tiny pin-pricks. There was a strong feeling that an offensive should be mounted to break through the Bar-Lev Line, push the Israelis back a few miles and inflict on them some 20,000 or more casualties, which would be far more seriously felt in a small country than in Egypt, and that any Egyptian casualties would be worth the end result. The Soviet military mission did what it could to hinder and dampen down such an adventurous idea, and the general staff hesitated, feeling that Israeli air superiority would nullify any such offensive, as the new Egyptian air force was not yet ready to take the air in sufficient strength to give it a reasonable chance of success. A disastrous failure on this scale would be a serious setback. Despite this many officers continued to press for a 'summer confrontation', and one of them later said to me: 'The Suez Canal might just as well be the Atlantic Ocean—it is such a barrier'. Practically all Egyptian officers now firmly believed that if Marshal Amer had been allowed to have his way and launch a pre-emptive attack on Israel in early June 1967 the Egyptian army in the Sinai would have been victorious.

On the night of the 29th April the Israelis mounted their second deep penetration raid into the Upper Nile Valley, claiming it to be a reprisal for 'uninterrupted provocations' by the Egyptians along the Suez Canal to make them aware that acts of aggression cannot continue without a 'proper answer'. Israeli commandos were flown into Egypt in helicopters, their targets being the Idfu bridge and dam, about 60 miles north of Aswan, and the transformer at Nag Hamadi (which had been attacked the previous October). It was claimed damage was caused and that all returned safely. However, the Egyptians said that there had been no helicopter landings on Egyptian soil that night, and that only one Israeli plane had neared the quoted targets, but had been driven off by anti-aircraft fire and forced to jettison its bomb-load without serious damage. Foreign journalists were taken to Nag Hamadi the following day, where there was no damage to be seen. This was one of the few instances where an Israeli claim had been seen to be over-stated. When addressing workers at Helwan on the 1st May, Nasser boasted that this Israeli raid had been a complete failure.

The same pattern, of daylight artillery and mortar barrages across the Canal, alternating with raids by Egyptian commandos by night, continued during May, particularly heavy shelling occurring along the whole length of the waterway on the 11th and 12th. Early in the month, for the first time the Israelis directed artillery fire on to Port Said, now completely evacuated by civilians. Military casualties were caused, but the Egyptian counter-claim was that in firing back their guns killed seven Israeli soldiers and two civilian tractor drivers. The Israelis also made a few commando raids, but not as many as the Egyptians, who on the 14th claimed to have foiled an Israeli attempt to cross in rubber boats. Moshe Dayan said he doubted that Israel would remain on the defensive if the war of attrition continued, commenting (on the 12th) that 'An army can be forced into an offensive war even if it doesn't want one'. Later, on the 28th, he warned Israeli students that the present 30-month conscription period of service might have to be increased. Just under 400 incidents along the Canal were logged by the UN observers during May. For example, four Israeli soldiers were wounded on the 26th, when their vehicle ran over a mine just north of Kantara.

The Soviet military mission began to disapprove of Egyptian shelling on such a scale across the Canal. Nasser was urged to order his armed forces to respect the cease-fire, but despite brave words and an attempt at continuing military independence, there were hesitation and uncertainty in the Egyptian camp. The Russians knew that although the Egyptian army had considerably improved in training and morale, and was satisfactorily absorbing Soviet equipment, it was not capable of undertaking an assault crossing in the face of Israeli opposition, and even less capable of competing with them in mobile warfare. Although the Soviet Union seemed prepared to send endless supplies of artillery and mortar ammunition, perhaps appreciating why Nasser was permitting barrages and commando raids, it was tardy in sending other items, such as jeeps, four-wheel drive trucks and amphibious vehicles—all essential for an offensive. Egyptian officers forever complained that the Russians only taught them about defence, and nothing whatever about mobile warfare or the set-piece attack.

Nasser knew that his army could not successfully march eastwards, and so he ostensibly remained in the Radda, or retaliation, phase of his strategy against Israel. Quoting the Soviet concept of defence by attrition, he declared that he was fighting an 'inch by inch' war. His opinion was faithfully echoed by Editor Heikal, who wrote in *Al Ahram* that if the Israelis wanted to take Cairo they would simply be absorbed, that they were already over-extended, and that a 'fourth round' would be a six year war and not a six day one. The Egyptian general staff felt by the end of May 1969 that an Israeli pre-emptive attack would not succeed, and that even if the Israelis managed to cross the Canal in force, they would be bogged down in the desert on the western side by prolonged resistance by the armed forces and the people. The Soviet military mission was content to accept this opinion.

It seemed almost as though Nasser had become a moderate, or would have dearly liked to be able to become one, but he was imprisoned by his own propaganda. He was apparently seeking to avoid a 'fourth round' and to find a way out of the situation of 'semi-war' in which he found himself. It was suspected that he was veering towards compromise in this respect. When interviewed,[1] in answer to a question as to whether he was ready to accept the existence of Israel if there were a withdrawal from the occupied territories and a permanent peace settlement, he replied: 'I accept the reality of Israel, and so will my people, if there is a humanitarian solution. Call it Israel, or whatever they want to call it, and I will recognize it'. But this was aimed at the American people, and not at the Egyptians. Nasser felt that the Russians were pressing him to make widespread concessions in their efforts to achieve a Middle East settlement in the Big Four talks, so that Moscow and Washington could reach an agreement and so ease the cold war. In Egypt one could detect traces of war-weariness appearing, and also irritation at having to carry the 'main burden' of the Arab war against the Israelis, which most Egyptians were under the impression they were doing, and there must have been many unspoken thoughts that a separate peace with Israel would be welcome. The budget, of nearly £200 million, 15 per cent higher than the previous year, giving priority 'to requirements of battle', was a wearisome burden.

Big Four talks continued and on the 10th June Gromyko, the Soviet Foreign Minister, went to Cairo, but he was received rather coolly as the Egyptians suddenly felt that the Russians were holding out by not encouraging them to attack Israel and by not supplying

[1] By Hedley Donovan, Editor-in-Chief of *Time*.

more items essential to an offensive. This situation caused Editor Heikal to assert that psychological warfare was being used to try to split the Egyptians and the Russians. So far the Soviet Union had not objected to Egyptians and Israelis trying to work out new borders for themselves, but now Gromyko changed this policy, and firmly demanded a total Israeli withdrawal from the occupied territories, and also demilitarized zones astride such new frontiers, which the Israelis had always resisted. The Egyptians now felt a little better, while the Israelis became gloomy. On the 12th, Israeli Navy Day, Moshe Dayan said that it was no longer certain if the Suez Canal were the cease-fire line or the front where the next war would begin.

The Israelis feared that if the Big Four powers came to an agreement they would be able to force a withdrawal from the occupied territories. Already they had lost 700 killed since the June War, and Dayan commented that 'hardly a night passes without a battle'. They felt that if left alone by the Big Four they would be able to force the Arabs eventually to come to an agreement with them, but they remained intransigent in that they never stated exactly how much of the occupied territories they intended to keep. Premier Golda Meir merely commented that the new frontiers 'must provide no natural advantage to our neighbours'. Most Israelis would have liked to have seen Nasser displaced, as they distrusted him so much, reflecting their Government's suspicions.

The Israeli general staff were concerned that Nasser seemed to believe his intelligence reports that stated that some 60 per cent of the Bar-Lev Line had been destroyed, when in fact Egyptian barrages had done comparatively little damage. This had caused Moshe Dayan to say (on the 18th May) that he did 'not think we shall reach that point [of full scale land fighting]—not this summer'. On the 5th June Egyptian Defence Minister Fawzi called for 'preparation for the decisive battle', adding that experience had shown that the enemy was not invincible. Despite feelings of frustration, the Egyptians thought that they were at least compelling the Israelis to fight their kind of war, in which big guns and big battalions counted most, and although behind in technology they hoped in this way to achieve a position of strength and dominance sufficient to force on the Israelis a peace settlement to their liking. The quest for more arms continued, and on the 15th June Premier Meir flew to London to try to persuade

E 65

the British Government to supply her with the new Chieftain tank. On the same day Ali Sabry flew to Moscow to try to persuade the Russians to step up arms deliveries. Both were unsuccessful.

U Thant's report to the UN said that there had been some reduction of violence along the Canal in the latter part of May, with less use of heavy weapons (but this was mainly limited to the northern section); that the improvement continued in the first week of June, and thereafter deteriorated, with shell fire almost daily; and that incidents were mainly commenced by the Egyptians. The same pattern of fighting continued. For example, on the 22nd June the Israelis admitted that four soldiers had been wounded by Egyptian commandos who had crossed the Canal near the Great Bitter Lakes. Two days later the Egyptians claimed that one of their commando units landed on the east bank for the second night in succession, crossing under cover of an artillery barrage and clashing with Israeli troops on the road to the Mitla Pass. They also claimed that on the same night, the 24th, another commando unit crossed and attacked Israeli positions at El Shatt, killing the occupants and destroying two armoured vehicles, saying that this was the fifth commando raid in three days, in which in all 22 Israeli soldiers had been killed for only two Egyptians wounded. On the 23rd an Egyptian commando raid just south of Kantara claimed to have killed 22 Israelis and destroyed installations, but the Israelis would admit to only one wounded. Other incidents during the month worth noting included the seizure by the Israelis on the 20th of an Egyptian motor vessel, with a crew of 19, in the Gulf of Suez. On the 27th, when the Israelis admitted three soldiers wounded in 24 hours, Moshe Dayan was forced to modify his previous prediction and say that 'war is drawing nearer'.

The Israelis also carried out a number of commando raids in June, but not as many as the Egyptians. The main one was on the night of the 21st, when naval commandos raided the Egyptian coastguard station at Ras Adabiya, in the Gulf of Suez, about six miles south of Suez town. They claimed to have killed about 15 soldiers manning it, and to have destroyed radar equipment and installations. The Egyptians would only admit to five killed and seven wounded, claiming in turn to have killed at least four Israelis and wounded others. The third Israeli deep penetration raid into the Upper Nile Valley was on the night of the 29th, when a group of commandos in helicopters raided Suhaj, about 90 miles from the Red Sea, and cut power cables. The Israelis said that no enemy was encountered, no shots were fired and there were no Israeli casualties. The ease with which this operation had been carried out caused Egyptian anxiety over the obvious vulnerability of the Upper Nile Valley.

On the 1st July Premier Meir uttered a biblical threat in the Knesset that 'Israel would hit back with seven blows for each one she received', while an Egyptian spokesman said: 'We consider ourselves at war', and admitted that more reserves were being mobilized. U Thant hinted that he might have to withdraw his 92 UN observers. On the 2nd Israeli commandos crossed the Canal in three separate landings and claimed to have killed 13 Egyptian soldiers. On the same day, as if to heighten tension, the Egyptians announced that an Israeli spy-ring had been discovered in Cairo, headed by Yusef Hamdan, a German of Egyptian origin, who with three others was arrested, one of whom was in possession of a classified map of the Egyptian Canal defences.

Claim and counter-claim continued throughout the month. On the 10th the Egyptians said that one of their raids had penetrated Israeli positions opposite Port Tewfik, causing 40 casualties for no Egyptian loss. In this instance the Israelis admitted that it had been 'relatively successful for the Egyptians', saying that six Israeli soldiers had been killed and that another died of wounds. On the 18th there were five Israeli casualties when a vehicle on the east bank struck a mine, and on the same day three Israeli soldiers were killed and five wounded in artillery exchanges across the Canal. By this time the number of Israelis killed amounted to about 70 a month. The Algerian brigade, positioned near Fayid, was active in commando raiding, using rubber boats to cross to lay mines and fix booby traps to vehicles.

On the night of the 19th July a group of about 40 Israeli naval commandos attacked Green Island, a fortified rock at the north end of the Gulf of Suez, buttressed by 25 feet high walls, having a radar tower and radar equipment and manned by about 70 Egyptian soldiers. Green Island had long been an irritation as it 'radar-controlled' the southern approach to the Suez Canal, and the northern part of the Gulf of Suez. The commandos scaled the walls, killed the sentries, destroyed equipment and then withdrew after being on the island for an hour. Thinking they were still there, the Egyptians on the mainland continued to bombard Green Island after they had left, causing more damage. The Egyptians claimed that the attempt had failed, that the Israelis lost 30 killed and that one Mirage fighter plane was brought down, as against six Egyptian casualties. The Israelis said that they killed 25 Egyptians.

5 · Aerial Conflict

'It will be a generation before Egyptian skills equal those of the Israelis'

Brigadier MORDACAI HOD, Israeli Air Force Commander

The air forces of both sides now come more fully into the war. On the afternoon of the 20th July 1969,[1] a few hours after the Israelis had raided Green Island, their planes began heavily to pound Egyptian guns along the side of the Suez Canal. Unlike Israeli guns, Egyptian guns were mainly 'towed', only a small proportion being self-propelled; on the Soviet concept they had tended to be static, settling down in fixed positions, 'hardened' by concrete and sandbagged blast walls and shelters as protection against Israeli shells and mortar bombs. So far the Israelis had generally been content to reply to the Egyptian barrages in kind, but as they had continued increasingly to extract a toll of Israeli casualties, the Israelis were provoked into a change of tactics. The 20th July marked the beginning of this phase of the war, when the main weight of the Israeli air force was turned on to the Egyptian front line weapons.

Just before dusk on that day the Egyptian air force flew out to challenge the Israeli air force seriously for the first time since the June War. About 40 aircraft (ten MiG-21s and 30 SU-7s) penetrated over 60 miles into the Sinai. Israeli aircraft were scrambled and a number of dog fights took place. When it was over the Egyptians claimed to have shot down 19 Israeli planes, but admitted the loss of two of their own, while the Israelis also admitted losing two planes but claimed to have brought down five Egyptian ones, listed as two SU-7s, two MiG-17s and one MiG-21. To the Israelis, who seemed to have won this air clash, the startling fact was that the Egyptian air force had penetrated in such strength so far into Israeli air space.

On the 23rd President Nasser, addressing the ASU on the 17th

[1] The Egyptians allege that the Israelis chose the same day as the American moon-landing, so as to attract minimum publicity overseas.

69

anniversary of the Egyptian revolution, described the air battle as the biggest clash since the June War, and gave his 'great appreciation and the people's satisfaction for the great effort and excellent results achieved in a day of great battles', but warned that it was a serious escalation of the fighting. Calling again for a war of attrition, he said: 'We are now engaged in a long battle to drain the enemy's strength . . . We are now beginning the stage of liberation . . . The Six Day War has not ended, but the two-, three- and even six-year war is continuing . . . We are still at war with the Israelis'.

The action by the Egyptian air force on the 20th was elatedly regarded by the Egyptians as the sign of its rehabilitation, and was seen as proof of Egyptian ability to carry out air strikes on Israeli targets despite losses, but it had been a long haul and there was still much to be done. The Israeli pre-emptive strike had caught the Egyptian air force off guard, and it had suffered heavily, losing in all about 300 combat planes out of 450, the majority in the first hours of the war. Through rapid growth and expansion it had always been handicapped by a chronic shortage of pilots, and in the June War at least 100 were killed and 250 wounded, leaving less than 100 fit for flying duty—hardly enough to man the remaining combat planes. In dog fights Israeli pilots had demonstrated their superiority.

General Mohammed Sidky, the Air Force Commander, had been dismissed for its failure in the June War. On the 11th June 1967 Lieutenant-General Madkour Abu al-Izz was appointed in his place, who together with other newly promoted and newly appointed senior officers set about reorganizing and rebuilding the air force with Soviet assistance. The trial of the four senior air force officers, and the resulting storm of protest caused by the leniency, have been mentioned. In the wave of recrimination other officers in executive positions were dismissed, until the Soviet military mission stepped in and prevented the removal of any more competent officers, in fact insisting that some who had done well on Soviet courses of instruction, or had shown their efficiency, were brought back; in this way a complete collapse of the command and executive structure of the air force was avoided.

One of the cardinal mistakes had been to concentrate their aircraft openly on just a few airfields within Israeli reach, and so the first phase had been to salvage all aircraft possible. Any plane that was recoverable or repairable was sent to other airfields beyond Israeli reach, as had been all aircraft that could fly. Those hastily diverted to the Yemen in unopened crates in the June War were brought back to Egypt. Soviet replacement aircraft, mainly crated MiG-21s, were soon arriving at the Cairo International airport, until by the end of August, according to Israeli estimates, about 60 per cent of the Egyptian June War losses had been replaced, which would number nearly 200 planes but would almost certainly include those crated aircraft which had been temporarily dispersed to the Yemen. Aircraft deliveries then slowed down almost to a stop, the Russians reasoning perhaps that there was no point in sending any more until Egyptian pilots were trained and available to fly them.

The Egyptians had lost five airfields when they were driven from the Sinai, being left with about 20 in Egypt, of which about two-thirds were within Israeli reach, and plans were made for the construction of about 15 more, mainly in the Delta area and the Nile Valley. The policy now was to have small concrete hangars for each individual plane, in which it remained when it was not flying, but this of course took months to complete. Five new airstrips were made between Cairo and Alexandria by simply asphalting over the central reservation of the dual-carriageway road.

To remedy the acute shortage of Egyptian pilots intensive courses, both in the Soviet Union and in Egypt, were organized to train more. Within weeks about 300 were in training, but it was many months before they were able to be launched into combat. The strength of the air force remained about the 20,000 mark throughout, but the number of pilots steadily, although very slowly, rose, as to the survivors of the June War were added wounded pilots as they recovered, who were joined by newly-fledged ones on completing their training. About 100 Soviet flying instructors were in Egypt for this purpose, with another 100 being integrated into the air force in executive, administrative, training and operational capacities, right through the organization, there being at least one Soviet adviser in each air squadron. On the 1st July 1967 Egyptian planes were again active in the skies of the Yemen in support of the brief final Egyptian offensive, after which the war there subsided until the Khartoum conference, when the Egyptians disengaged, and all planes and pilots were brought home to be integrated into the new air force that was slowly forming.

Urged on them by the Soviet military mission was the policy of self-preservation, which neatly fitted into Nasser's Samud phase of his strategy, of standing fast and not admitting defeat. It was a survival stage, so the air force was kept in the background and away from the enemy as much as possible, while the work of conserving, accumulating and rebuilding a new air force able to defeat the Israeli air force in battle went on. Pilots were scarce and not expendable; they were kept away from the Canal zone and forbidden to intercept any Israeli aircraft that occasionally flew over Egypt just after the June War to demonstrate their freedom of the skies above that country. On the other hand, Israeli aircraft generally kept to the Canal Zone and away from the Delta, Cairo and the Nile Valley. Early in December 1967 a squadron of 10 Soviet TU-16 bombers went to Cairo to 'show the flag', staying for some days, which gave the Israelis the hint that Soviet air power was in the offing and capable of intervening if thought necessary. In April, the following year, another Soviet air squadron visited Egypt for the same purpose, and there were other similar visits on later dates.

Despite the crushing defeat the morale of the Egyptian pilots remained steady and many felt that they never had a chance to prove themselves. Before the June War their morale and confidence had been high, and they had been praised by their Soviet instructors; they had no reason to accept that they were inferior, and their spirits were kept up on this belief. A few venturesome Egyptian pilots flew into the Canal Zone, at times it is suspected against orders, and more credit should be given to them for their courage in facing the known superiority of the Israeli air force. On the 4th July 1967 the Israelis claimed to have shot down a low-flying Egyptian plane near Port Tewfik, and to have driven off a second one by anti-aircraft fire. On the 8th four Egyptian MiGs appeared over the east bank of the Canal, the Israelis claiming to have shot down one when it was nine miles inside Israeli air space; after that Egyptian pilots seem to have been kept on a tighter leash.

Conversely, on the 25th October 1967, the day after the oil refineries at Port Suez had been set on fire for the first time by Israeli heavy mortars, the Air Force Commander was dismissed for not scrambling his planes and using them against the Israeli gunners. This made the eager Egyptian pilots feel better, and may have been a sop to them, as had Egyptian aircraft taken off they would have fallen into a trap and been pounced upon by waiting Israeli planes hovering overhead, when the end result could only have been greater Egyptian loss. The dismissed commander was replaced by Lieutenant-General Mustafa al-Hennawi, who was reputed to be a good organizer and a sound administrator.

It was largely upon the insistence of the Soviet advisers that the Egyptian pilots were held back from action; they thought that the Egyptians should study, practise, train and work harder, and that it would be another two or three years before they would be ready to challenge the Israelis in the air successfully. This caused resentment amongst impatient pilots, which came to a head in early December 1967, when the Israelis were discovered constructing a landing strip in the Sinai near the Great Bitter Lakes. The pilots wanted to bomb it, but were refused permission, and so they staged a sit-down strike which lasted for four days.

Concerned at the cessation of aircraft deliveries from the Soviet Union, when he was in Moscow in July 1968 President Nasser asked for, amongst other items, more combat aircraft, and was promised some MiG-21s and SU-7s. Already, according to Israeli estimates, about 80 per cent of Egypt's June War losses had been replaced, and any further deliveries would bring the strength of its air force up to the pre-June War level of about 450 combat planes.

The Egyptian Air Force did make the occasional sortie, mainly for reconnaissance purposes, which also brought about an occasional clash between hostile aircraft. On the 31st October 1968, for example, the day after the Israeli raid on Nag Hamadi, two Egyptian MiGs were involved in a dog fight with two Israeli Mirages over the Canal, each side claiming to have shot down one of the other's planes, which each denied. After this MiGs made practice scrambles over Cairo at intervals, but no Israeli planes appeared.

The Nag Hamadi raid caused anxiety for the security of the Aswan Dam and towns and irrigation works in the Upper Nile Valley, where about two-thirds of the population lived, being engaged in agriculture along the narrow strip of irrigated land on either side of the river. Severe damage to canals and control dams could endanger life and property on a large scale. It was realized that there were gaps in the Egyptian air defences, which themselves were vulnerable, owing to Israeli aircraft being able to fly below the defensive radar beams to get through to their target. Defences were built up around the Aswan Dam that included SAM-2s and radar-directed 57mm anti-aircraft guns, some manned by Russians. The Egyptians hoped that this would deter the Israelis from attacking in case they should cause Soviet casualties and so become involved in an international incident. Later, Soviet-manned SAM-3s were added to the defences around the Aswan Dam, which in theory had the capability of bringing down the Israeli-piloted Mirages and Phantoms.

President Nasser launched his war of attrition in the early spring of 1969, when he authorized the recommencement of heavy artillery barrages and commando raids across the Canal, all of which made the impatient air force rather restive. Although the Russians did not think it was yet ready to face the Israelis, a number of sorties were allowed in the Canal Zone, commencing in May, and inevitably a few clashes occurred. On the 24th, for example, there was an aerial battle near Kantara, when both sides made contrary claims. The Egyptians said that three formations of Israeli aircraft tried to enter Egyptian air space, but were driven back with the loss of one Israeli plane, while the Israelis stated that two Egyptian formations tried to cross the Canal, that their aircraft brought down two planes in the fighting, and that a HAWK missile accounted for a third. The HAWK missile hit a MiG-21 flying at 22,000 feet, destroying a plane of this type for the very first time.

In June there was another clash on the 2nd, over the Gulf of Suez, when in a 20-minute battle the Israelis said that their planes shot down four Egyptian MiGs, while the Egyptians claimed to have downed two Israeli planes while all theirs returned to base safely. On the 17th, as a warning and to remind the Egyptians of the length of their reach, the Israelis sent a few planes on a flight over Cairo, practically the first since immediately after the June War, but they had departed when the Egyptians belatedly scrambled their MiGs. Later in the month, on the 26th, the Israelis claimed to have shot down four Egyptian MiGs, while the Egyptians said that they brought down two Israeli aircraft, which was denied. In another clash, on the 7th July, the Israelis said that they had shot down two MiG-21s, south of Sharm el Sheikh; while the Egyptians admitted the air battle, they denied any loss.

This brings us up to the air battle of the 20th July 1969. Although President Nasser gave his nation a glowing account of this action, on the 24th he dismissed both General Mustafa al-Hennawi, the Air Force Commander, and General Mohammed Ali Fahmi, the Air

Defence Commander, replacing them with Major-Generals Ali Baghdadi and Hassan Kamel respectively. The interpretation put on these two major changes of appointment was that while Hennawi and Fahmi were regarded as good organizers, they had completed their task of basically reforming the air force and the air defence, and that now it was time for someone else to instil fighting spirit into them ready for the battles ahead.

By mid-1969 Egypt possessed about 350 combat aircraft, all current Soviet models, most quite modern, which were roughly about the same number as Israel had. Although estimates vary slightly, mainly perhaps because of the slow but continuing rate of delivery of certain planes being geared to the availability of trained Egyptian pilots to fly them, by types they probably consisted of about 100 MiG-21s, 120 MiG-17s and 19s, 85 SU-7s, 15 TU-16s and 30 Il-28s. While it is not necessary to become too technical, a brief description of them and their capabilities is of interest.

The MiG[1] series were developments of the original MiG-15, a single seat jet fighter which made its appearance on the Communist side in the Korean War in 1950. The MiG-17 was simply an improved version, having two 23mm cannon, but the MiG-19 was faster, being a twin-engined fighter armed with two 37mm and two 23mm cannon, and the first of its kind to fly supersonic in level flight. The MiG-21 was the most modern fighter the Egyptians possessed, which in addition to cannon also carried two air-to-air 150-lb missiles, having a range of about two miles and an infra-red homing guidance system, being somewhat identical in performance to the American Sidewinder. The MiG-21 was considered to be the technical match for the Israelis' Super-Mystères. While fast and manoeuvrable the MiGs were very short range planes, the MiG-21 having one of only 200 miles, and the other models less, which meant that they must be positioned close to the battle area, and were only able to stay in the air for limited periods. Nasser had asked for the improved MiG-21J, and also for the later MiG-23, but had not been successful.

The SU-7, of the Sukhoi series,[2] the basic tactical attack aircraft in the Soviet air force, was a single-seat, swept wing fighter-bomber

---

[1] Compounded from the initial letters of its two designers, Mikoyan and Gurevich.

[2] Sukhoi, Tupolev, Ilyushin, Antonov and Mil are all names of Soviet aircraft designers.

with two 30mm cannon, a speed of Mach 1·5, and able to carry both bombs and rockets, but now the Israelis occupied the Sinai, Israel was beyond their reach. The TU-16, of the Tupolev series,[1] was a medium reconnaissance bomber, able to carry a bomb load of 20,000lb, having a crew of seven, seven 23mm cannon, the rear two being radar-controlled, and a range of over 2,000 miles. Carrying Soviet air-to-air missiles, it was feared by the Israelis as it could reach every part of their country. The 30 TU-16s, possessed by the Egyptians in 1967, were the first targets in the June War, when all were caught on the ground at the Beni Suef and Luxor airfields and destroyed. The Il-28, of the Ilyushin series[1], was a light twin jet-engined bomber, able to carry a bomb load of up to 10,000 lb, with a radius of action of 850 miles. The aircraft were grouped into squadrons, there being six of interceptor-fighters with MiG-21s, four of fighters of MiG-19s, two of fighters of MiG-17s, five of ground attack aircraft, with SU-7s one of heavy bombers of TU-16s, and two of light bombers of Il-28s.

Of other aircraft possessed by Egypt, worth mentioning and not included in the 350 combat planes, were about 40 Il-14s, a piston-engined light transport aircraft, carrying six passengers or 1,300 lb freight, and about 20 An-12s, of the Antonov series,[1] transport aircraft, able to carry up to 44,000 lb or 100 troops, with a range of about 1,000 miles, which could take vehicles. On the training side there were about 150 older aircraft, mainly MiGs, Yaks and Delfin trainers. It should be pointed out that it is difficult to assess generally the radius of action of aircraft, especially bombers and helicopters, as so much depends upon the load they are carrying, and such factors as whether extra fuel tanks are on board or fixed below the wings, but the ranges where quoted are those for a full payload to the target at the extreme distance from base.

Egypt also had about 70 helicopters of various types in the Mikhail L Mil series,[1] the Mi-1 being one of the earliest utility ones; the Mi-4, able to lift a payload of 3,800 lb or 11 troops had a range of 150 miles; the Mi-6, the largest helicopter in the world, had a payload of 40,000 lb, able to lift 70 soldiers, having a crew of five and a range of 200 miles; and the Mi-8, a transport helicopter, was able to lift 28 soldiers, having a payload of 6,600 lb and a range of 240 miles.

The air defence of Egypt was built around anti-aircraft guns and

[1] See footnote 2 on page 75.

SAM batteries, co-ordinated by radar, and the six squadrons of MiG-21 interceptor fighters; as it was not possible to be strong everywhere, the Egyptians had concentrated their resources around Cairo, Alexandria, the Delta and the Aswan Dam. The low-level aircraft attacks were to be dealt with by the anti-aircraft guns, which included modern Soviet ones of 37mm, 57mm, 85mm and 100mm calibres, many radar-operated, some twin-barrelled and some capable of firing up to 180 rounds per minute at ranges up to 10,000 feet.

The SAM-2 missiles[1] had been the backbone of the standard air defence system of the Soviet Union, and were designed to combat aircraft flying at medium and high altitudes. It was a two-stage missile, with a high explosive warhead weighing 288 lb, a 'slant range' of 28 miles and a ceiling of about 60,000 feet. The target was tracked by radar, and the missile had an automatic radio command guidance system. It was not very effective against fast, low-flying aircraft, being slow to get off the launching pad and slow to accelerate initially. The SAM-2 had not proved effective against Israeli aircraft in the June War, and had given disappointing results in Vietnam. Since the June War a few more had been received, and by mid-1969 Egypt probably had about 200 or slightly more. The missiles were in a separate command, firmly under Soviet control, the Soviet adviser with the battery having the firing fuse, although they were manned and serviced by Egyptian personnel. They were formed into 25 batteries, each of six launchers, and were deployed around Cairo, Alexandria, certain major airfields such as Cairo West and Inshas, the Aswan Dam and in the Canal Zone. The SAM-2 was mobile on its launcher, but could not be fired on the move, and was best operated from a circular concrete standing, which was conspicuous to Israeli aircraft. Immediately prior to the June War Egypt had about 150 SAM-2 missiles scattered on about 18 sites, one of which was in the Sinai, and was captured intact by the Israelis, who accordingly became familiar with it.

Regarded as the key to their victory in the June War, the highly trained Israeli air force had knocked out that of Egypt within hours, destroyed that of Jordan within the hour, and so badly mauled those of Syria and Iraq that they kept their distance. At the

[1] SAM means Surface-to-Air Missile; the Soviet designation for the missile is V750VK, and for the whole system V78SM, while the NATO code name is Guideline.

commencement of the war Israel possessed about 450 planes of all sorts, of which about 350 were combat aircraft, and in the fighting about 40 were lost. Since its inception as a state, Israel had experienced great difficulty in obtaining aircraft and in building up an air force at all, and it was really not until 1958, when it found a friend in France (then deeply involved with insurrection in Algeria, and perhaps because Egypt was assisting the insurgents), that Israel was able to obtain French planes in some number and so expand its air force to a size adequate for its defence. At the start of the June War Israel had about 20 Super Mystères, 40 Mystères Mark IVa, 73 Mirages Mark IIIJ, 48 Ouragans, 60 Fouga Magisters, 25 Vatour IIAs, 20 Noratlas and Stratocruiser transport aircraft and about 25 helicopters. Most of the planes had a range of 400 miles or less, and were grouped into 13 squadrons, there being four of interceptors, five of fighter-bombers, two of transport and two of helicopters.

The first west European craft capable of supersonic speeds in level flight, the Super Mystère was the fastest and most modern aircraft possessed by the Israelis and considered to be a technical match for the MiG-21. A fighter-bomber, it was fitted with rockets, could carry napalm tanks and had two 30mm cannon. The Mystère IVA was an older (French production had ceased in 1958) turbo-jet, ground attack fighter, carrying both bombs and napalm tanks, with two 30mm cannon. The obsolescent Ouragan was the oldest fighter-bomber in Israeli service, having four 20mm cannon and able to carry a bomb-load of over 2,000 lb. The Vatours, twin engined, single-seat, all weather, multi-mission, ground attack bombers, were able to carry a bomb-load of 4,000 lb, and were also comparatively old.

The single-seat Mirage Mark IIIs, first delivered to Israel in 1963, were the only Israeli interceptor capable of challenging the MiG-21s. They were delta-wing, supersonic, multi-mission fighters, with two 30mm cannon, a speed of Mach 2·1, able to operate from short and rough airstrips. The Fouga Magisters, assembled in Israel, were tandem two-seat trainers, strengthened and modified to carry bombs, rockets and napalm tanks, and were used in a ground support role. Two French missiles were in service with the Israeli air force. One was the Matra R530 air-to-air missile, having a 60-lb high explosive warhead, a range of 11 miles and an infra-red homing system, which were the standard armament on Mystères, Mirages and Vatours. The other was the Nord AS30, an air-to-ground missile, with a high explosive warhead of about 500 lb, with a heat-homing device.

Of the other aircraft mentioned, the Noratlas, the French Nord 2501, was a medium transport craft, able to carry 45 soldiers and to take vehicles loaded through a rear door. The American Strato-cruiser, the Boeing 377, was also able to carry personnel and freight. The Super Frelon, the French Sud 321, was a medium sized, general purpose helicopter, able to carry a payload of 9,000 lb, or 30 soldiers, having a crew of two and a range of over 300 miles. The Sikorski UH-34 was a scaled up version of the Sikorski 55, which had been used in the Korean War, a utility helicopter able to lift 18 soldiers, with a range of 280 miles. It was also known as the Sikorski-58. The French Alouette was a small reconnaissance helicopter, with a payload of 1,400 lb, able to carry the pilot and four passengers and having a range of less than 200 miles. It will be seen that the aircraft in use with the Israeli air force were predominantly French.

The strength of the regular element of the Israeli air force was about 8,000, and could be expanded to about 20,000 on full mobilization, of whom about 1,200 were pilots on regular engage-ments, whose average age was about 24 years and who had commenced flying at the age of 18. They flew at least 24 hours a month, as against 12–16 in most other air forces and less in the Egyptian air force. Great emphasis was placed in pilot training on low flying and accurate cannon shooting at ground targets. The ground crew specialized in a quick 'turn round' time for the aircraft; this was reduced to about ten minutes, as opposed to at least half an hour in most other air forces, which enabled the Israelis to fly many more sorties. Serviceability of aircraft was high. The Israelis operated from about 20 airfields in Israel, including the Negev, and they had acquired five others when they overran the Sinai. Since then they had constructed over half-a-dozen desert landing strips to back up the Bar-Lev Line.

The Israeli pilots had one big advantage over the Egyptians, in that they had made up a 'Soviet squadron' of five Soviet aircraft, consisting of one SU-7, three MiG-17s and one MiG-21, which was used in training to familiarize them with the capabilities of the planes they might encounter in action. The SU-7 had been shot down in the 20th July 1969 battle, and had landed on soft sand; of the

MiG-17s, two had been landed in Israel by mistaken Iraqi pilots, while one shot down was able to be repaired, and the MiG-21 was acquired when an Iraqi pilot defected.

Israel possessed HAWK (Homing All the Way Killer) missiles, which were under the command of the air force, each battery having six triple-launchers. Israel had about 50 launchers, and a number were deployed along the Bir Gifgafa ridge. Developed by the Americans in 1960, the HAWK had a 'slant range' of 22 miles; it had recorded successes at heights from 100 feet to 38,000 feet, and it could also be used against ground targets. Its great advantage was that its 'continuous wave radar' could distinguish the echo of a fast-moving target from the general 'background clatter'.

Although after the June War the Israelis dominated the skies of the Middle East, the far-sighted Government and general staff looked to the future, being anxious about replacements for the war losses and wanting to obtain more aircraft to retain their dominant position, but the future in this respect seemed dismal. During the June War President de Gaulle, formerly considered by the Israelis as their one true ally and source of sophisticated aircraft, had unexpectedly come down on the side of the Arabs, condemning the Israelis for their actions and placing a total embargo on French arms to Israel, to the great dismay of all Israelis. Israel had ordered, and paid for in advance, 50 Mirage Vs, on which they were relying to form their interceptor squadrons of the near future. They never did, in fact, receive these planes, and had great difficulty in getting their money back.

The French would not relent, so in January 1968 Premier Eshkol went to America to try to persuade President Johnson to supply modern aircraft to Israel, asking, according to press reports, for 50 Phantoms, America's most advanced operational plane at that time, to make up for the embargoed French Mirages. Eshkol also asked for the delivery of Skyhawks, ordered in 1966, to be speeded up, none having yet been received in Israel. But the American President was hesitant, and Eshkol went away empty-handed. Johnson, however, had some second thoughts and three months later deliveries of the Skyhawk to Israel commenced.

The Douglas A4 Skyhawk was a single-seat attack bomber that had been in service with the US Navy since 1956, being designed to operate from naval carriers and short airfields. Having turbo-jet engines, two 20mm cannon, with a range of 1,200 miles, it carried bombs and the American Sidewinder air-to-air missile. The Side-winder had a 10-lb high explosive warhead, a range of two miles, a speed of Mach 2·5, and an infra-red homing guidance system. The only other aircraft obtained by Israel in 1968 were about 20 Italian Agusta Bell utility helicopters having a range of about 260 miles.

President Johnson had more second thoughts. On the 9th October it was announced in America that negotiations would begin for the sale of US Phantoms to Israel, a decision that caused President Nasser to deduce that America had decided to place the onus of defence directly on Israel and was about to abandon its responsibility in the Big Four guarantees to the Middle East; but it was not so. It was simply that President Johnson had delayed authorization for several months in the hope that the Soviet Union would be equally restrained in its supplies of arms to Egypt and other Middle East Arab countries.

The twin-engined, twin-seat, multi-mission McDonnell F-4B Phantom entered US Naval service in 1962, and was able to fly at Mach 2·4 speed, operate at 71,000 feet, and carry seven tons of either bombs, rockets, napalm or extra fuel tanks. In addition to its 20mm cannon it carried the Sparrow air-to-air missile, which had a con-tinuous-wave, semi-active radar homing system, with an all-weather, all-altitudes capability, a range of eight miles, a speed of Mach 2·5, and weighed about 60 lb. Vietnam experience had shown that this aircraft could absorb heavy damage and still return to base. The Phantom also carried the anti-radar Shrike missile, having a solid-propellant motor, a range of about 10 miles and a conventional high explosive warhead.

Because French helicopters had been used by the Israelis in their raid on Beirut airport on the 28th December 1968, when they destroyed 11 Arab airliners, President de Gaulle placed a total embargo on arms to Israel, which spelt final doom for the 50 Mirages, as well as three helicopters, aircraft spares and electronic equipment on order. Although practically all aircraft in service with the Israeli air force were French, they were not quite as badly off as they might have been, as when the June War embargo had been relaxed in the following September they had obtained large quantities of aircraft and other spares, and so had reserves. Their home arms industry was busily making them as well. This blow was in any case offset by a change in American policy, and on the day after the Palestinian guerilla action at Athens airport (on the 26th December 1968), and the day before the Israeli raid on Beirut airport, the US State Department announced that agreement had been reached for the sale of 50 Phantoms to Israel, and that delivery would begin before the end of 1969 and continue on into 1970.

The two air forces were about to do battle with each other. On the one side was the Israeli air force, experienced, combat-tested, successful and confident, with high morale. On the other was the Egyptian air force, newly rebuilt, untested in battle, short of pilots, lacking experience, and perhaps over-confident with impatient pilots itching to prove their worth.

6 · Air Power Intervenes

'It would be absolutely wrong to conceal the shortcomings in the Egyptian army'

Pravda, of the 13th September 1969.

The Egyptian air force launched itself at the Israeli air force, and for just over a week attempted to combat it. After the initial attack on the 20th July, the next big clash occurred over the Canal on the 24th, when Israeli aircraft raided Egyptian positions and there was aerial fighting. When it was over the Israelis claimed to have shot down seven Egyptian planes in dog fights since the 20th, without loss to themselves, bringing their total claimed since the June War to 19,[1] while the Egyptians claimed to have shot down six Israeli aircraft, for the admitted loss of one SU-7.

On the next day, the 25th, there was another clash of aircraft over the Canal when Egyptian planes scrambled to meet Israeli ones attacking ground defences, and fighting developed. In the afternoon a formation of Egyptian planes penetrated into Sinai air space where it was opposed by Israeli fighters and HAWK missiles. The usual claims and counter-claims were made, but the Egyptians again disengaged. During the following two days there were several Israeli raids on Egyptian positions along the Canal, but only one serious Egyptian attempt was made to intercept them. On the 28th, when Israeli planes attacked Port Tewfik, the Egyptians claimed to have brought down one plane.

Although there was activity on the part of the Egyptian air force right until the last days of July, and afterwards, it realized that it had lost its three or four main battles in the air against the Israelis, and so disengaged to lick its wounds and reconsider tactics. On the 31st July, on television, Moshe Dayan said that the Egyptians had finally realized their inability to achieve the air superiority they required to cover a large scale offensive; their threats were less

[1] Being 5 MiG-17s, 10 MiG21s and 4 SU-7s.

deadly, and uttered with less conviction, than before. Dayan commented that 'Egyptian aircraft are based very far from the front line, but they are still within reach'. The Israeli general staff was relieved, as it had not been quite certain of the exact capability of the new Soviet-trained and Soviet-equipped Egyptian air force, but now it was satisfied that the Israelis retained their great superiority over it. However, July had been a peak month for Israeli casualties, there being 30 killed and 76 wounded on the Canal front.

The Egyptian general staff comforted itself with the thought that the air force had made a come-back; that it was effective despite loss; that another Israeli pre-emptive air strike could have no more than a 40 per cent chance of success; and that now the Egyptians possessed a 'second strike' capability. Distance from the battle area meant more limited time over the target or in aerial combat. In the air battles there was a predominance of MiG-17s and MiG-19s, planes inferior in technical performance to Israeli Mirages, but this had been a policy of necessity as Egypt had to use whatever pilots it had, most of whom were only qualified on those two models. The newer MiG-21 pilots were generally outclassed by the Israelis, although their aircraft were technically equal, which indicated their need of more experience.

The object of these aerial attacks on Egyptian guns along the Canal had been to relieve pressure on the Bar-Lev Line, which had only been achieved to a degree; Egyptian gun positions by this time were well protected and fortified and, despite harassment, the weapons were able to continue firing across the waterway, causing Israeli casualties,[1] although not to the same extent. A similar policy was carried on in August, the Israelis trying to eliminate Egyptian aircraft from the skies above the Canal by attacking any that showed its nose, while at the same time continuing to pound Egyptian guns and mortars heavily. The Israelis took full advantage of this respite to strengthen the Bar-Lev Line.

Generally August was a quiet month in the air, although on most days Israeli aircraft attacked Egyptian gun positions somewhere along the Canal. There was a big clash on the 19th, after Egyptians had shelled Israeli positions across from Port Tewfik, when Israeli aircraft (including numbers of the recently received American

[1] The Israelis said, on the 4th August 1969, that 189 Israelis had been killed on the Egyptian front since the June War.

Skyhawks) hit at Egyptian positions in that area and up to ten miles inland. The Egyptians claimed to have shot down three planes, and the Israelis admitted losing a Skyhawk, the pilot being taken prisoner. The first batch of about a dozen Israeli pilots had returned from America on the 9th August, where they had been training on Phantoms, and in the first days of September the first Phantom aircraft arrived in Israel, the date of delivery having been put forward because of the coup in Libya on the 1st September.

During September the pattern was much the same. On the 7th General Bar-Lev stated that since the 20th July, when the Israeli air force first intervened on the Canal front, it had carried out 1,000 sorties over Egyptian territory, losing three aircraft, as compared with 100 Egyptian sorties in which they lost 21 aircraft. These figures indicated that although the Egyptian effort was less than one-tenth of the Israelis', it was not entirely insignificant, but General Bar-Lev echoed the Defence Minister's opinion that the air actions in July had brought home to the Egyptians the fact that they did not have sufficient air strength or air protection to cover a ground offensive.

So far, in this phase, Israeli aircraft had concentrated mainly upon Egyptian weapon positions along the Canal side, but as the Israeli casualty list of ground troops grew still longer, they switched to attacking missile sites as well. On the 9th September, for example, in one of the first such raids, they made an air strike on the Soviet-controlled radar base at Ras Dareg, in the Gulf of Suez, and the following day, the 10th, they raided missile sites in the southern part of the Canal.

The Egyptian air force, which had been fairly quiet for some time, suddenly struck back on the 11th, when it mustered 102 planes and flew across the central part of the Canal into the Sinai, where they were met by Israeli fighter aircraft and HAWK missiles. A swirl of dog fights developed, the battle lasting for an hour until the Egyptians disengaged and turned for home. Admitting the loss of one plane when it was over, the Israelis claimed to have brought down 11 Egyptian aircraft (eight in combat, two by HAWK missiles and one by anti-aircraft fire), while the Egyptians said that the Israelis had lost three planes in dog fights and one by anti-aircraft fire, but admitted the loss of two of their own. While once again Israeli pilots proved superior, they saw that the Egyptian air force was becoming more experienced. On the 24th there were extremely heavy and selective air strikes against missile sites along the Canal.

In early October Moshe Dayan announced the start of a 'limited air offensive', which was to concentrate upon destroying missile sites and the Egyptian early warning system. Israeli aircraft began to attack radar installations, not only in the Canal Zone and in the Gulf of Suez but along the Mediterranean coast, reaching even west of Alexandria. The radars were quickly replaced and damage made good, but reports by Sudanese and Algerian officers indicated how successful some of these Israeli strikes had been. Foreigners were not allowed to travel along the road west from El Alamein without special permits. Other areas were also barred to them, some for normal military security reasons but others, it was suspected, to hide the extent of damage caused.

During October the Israelis carried out attacks on missile and radar sites, as well as engaging any Egyptian aircraft encountered, which were becoming bolder although no more successful. On the 6th there were air battles over the Canal, in which the Israelis claimed to have brought down three Egyptian planes, but the Egyptians admitted the loss of one only, saying that its pilot had parachuted to safety. More dog fights occurred during the following day, with ensuing claims and counter-claims. Also, on the 7th, Israeli aircraft struck at Ras Zafarana, in the Gulf of Suez, where Egyptians were rebuilding radar and other installations destroyed in an Israeli commando raid the previous month. On the 16th the Israelis claimed to have destroyed eight SAM-2 sites since the 1st September. On the 24th a group of Egyptian planes attacked Israeli positions and installations in the Romani area, about 20 miles east of the Canal and some two miles from the sea, in which 11 Israelis were wounded. Later that day the Israelis retaliated, aiming at targets in the central sector of the Canal, and dog fights developed as each tried to silence the other's guns.

On the 10th November an Israeli spokesman stated that all the SAM-2 sites along the Canal from Port Said to the Gulf of Suez had been destroyed in a two-month aerial campaign against them. The next day there was another air battle over the Canal, the Israelis claiming to have brought down three Egyptian fighters for no loss, while the Egyptians claimed two Israeli jets for the loss of one plane.

At a press conference on the 13th Moshe Dayan said that since the 1st April the Egyptians had carried out 13 air attacks on Israeli positions. More were to come, and on the 24th a formation of Egyptian aircraft bombed Israeli positions between Kantara and Balusa on the road eastwards, in retaliation, according to *Al Ahram*, for an Israeli raid the previous night in which 132 tons of bombs were dropped in four hours. Jargon tended to change, and the expression 'pre-emptive attack', coined by the Israelis in June 1967, fell out of use; neither did they speak of 'retaliatory attacks' any more, but instead of 'anticipatory counter-attacks'.

The next aerial battle occurred on the 27th November, when Israeli planes made heavy attacks on Canal positions, which provoked the Egyptians into sending a formation of aircraft eastwards into the Sinai, where it was met about 25 miles east of the Canal by Israeli fighters. Dog fights developed and there were the usual conflicting claims, but the Egyptians admitted losing one plane in the fighting and another by anti-aircraft fire. In December, on the 25th, the Israeli air force made its longest strike to date, of over eight hours' continuous pounding of missile and radar sites that were being constructed in a ten-mile wide belt in the central and southern sectors of the Canal Zone. The Israelis claimed that all new installations were destroyed, and that all their planes returned safely, but on the following day their air force was again out in strength on the same type of mission.

Summing up at the end of 1969, Moshe Dayan stated that the Israeli air force retained an almost unchallenged air supremacy by attacking Egyptian aircraft that ventured into the Sinai; it had destroyed 24 SAM-2 sites and brought down 61 Egyptian aircraft since the June War, which had contributed to lowering the Israeli casualty rate in the Bar-Lev Line. On the Egyptian side, it was an understatement to say that the Russians were alarmed at the ease with which Israeli aircraft dodged their missiles and destroyed SAM-2 sites.

Meanwhile other operations had been taking place. Looking back to the night of August the 27th 1969, an Israeli commando unit in Super-Frelon helicopters flew across Egypt to the Upper Nile Valley, landed and lobbed mortar bombs into the headquarters of the Egyptian southern front, at Mankabad, six miles west of the town of Asyut, which was about 165 miles from the southern entrance to the Gulf of Suez. No serious damage was done. Next, on the 7th September, Israeli naval commandos raided the Egyptian naval base at Ras as-Sadat, 12 miles south of Suez, Israeli frogmen destroying two MTBs in the small harbour. The Israelis suffered no loss in the raid, but on the return journey three were killed by an explosion in one of their craft.

On the 9th September the Israelis launched their largest and most audacious raid on the southern flank of Egyptian territory, which they afterwards referred to as the 'ten hour war'. In the early hours of the morning an Israeli convoy of MTBs and landing craft, carrying six tanks and three armoured personnel carriers (all Soviet vehicles captured in the Six Day War) with Egyptian identifications on them, steamed westwards across the Gulf of Suez. Also on board were about 150 Israeli commandos, all Arabic speakers, dressed in Egyptian uniforms. The vehicles and men landed at El Khafayer, about 25 miles south of Suez just after dawn without being suspected, and after destroying radar equipment began to move southwards along the main coastal road. Shortly after leaving El Khafayer the commandos met an Egyptian convoy of troops moving towards them, which unsuspectingly pulled to one side of the narrow roadway to let them pass, enabling the Israelis to machine-gun them as they sped by. By this time there was overhead protection in the form of Israeli aircraft, which was continuous and seldom less than 30 planes. Support was also given from the sea, Israeli naval craft moving southwards in line with the commandos, firing at sentries, destroying posts and installations as they went, and at the small port of Ras Dareg putting more radar equipment out of action.

In the afternoon the Israelis neared the small port of Ras Zafarana about 56 miles south of Suez, where more radar installations were destroyed. In this area the Israelis seized four new Soviet armoured vehicles, one of which at least was a T-62.[1] Ten hours after landing on Egyptian territory and motoring some 30 miles through it, the Israeli commandos re-embarked at Ras Zafarana, taking with them four new Soviet armoured vehicles, having only one man wounded in the course of the whole operation, but claiming to have killed at least 150 Egyptians. Later the Egyptians falsely claimed to have

---

[1] *Daily Express* of the 17th October 1969.

foiled the landing and to have inflicted heavy losses on the Israelis, which included sinking two Israeli ships and bringing down three planes. The excuse for not scrambling aircraft or mounting a counter-attack on land was that they did not want to expose their aircraft, vehicles and soldiers to the Israeli jets overhead waiting to pounce.

One of the main objects of the raid had been to demonstrate to the Soviet Union that no new secret equipment was safe with the Egyptians. Israeli intelligence had come to know of the presence of the Soviet T-62s, which the Egyptians were asking for in quantity, and one or two of them had been sent for trials, the Egyptians assuring the Russians that they would be absolutely safe from Israeli attack. The T-62 had come into service with the Soviet Army only in 1965, and had not been examined by Western experts. All that was known then was that it was a 37-ton tank with a 115mm gun, more heavily armoured than anything the Israelis possessed, and they were anxious to test its gun against their own armoured vehicles and their own anti-tank guns against the armour of the T-62.

The Israeli raid of the 9th September caused second thoughts in Egypt as the weakness and vulnerability of its southern front and the Upper Nile Valley were dramatically revealed. For some time there had been a continuing controversy within the general staff as to whether it was best to concentrate available forces and defensive resources around the major population centres, such as Cairo and Alexandria, and certain vital airfields, to be better able to repel any offensive against them, or whether to disperse men and arms over a wider area so as to be more favourably placed to combat Israeli strikes inland, and so give confidence to the people. Until the 9th September the school of thought favouring concentrating the defences, encouraged by the Russian advisers (who were influenced by the traditions of the defence of Moscow and other Soviet cities in World War II) had carried the day. Apart from the Suez Canal front, just a few cities and airfields were heavily defended on the rigid Soviet frontal pattern, consequently leaving the flanks, especially the southern one, exposed and weak. Now there was concern for the Aswan Dam and the Upper Nile Valley generally, most of which was little more than 150 miles from the Gulf of Suez or the Red Sea, and so well within range of Israeli commandos in long-range helicopters. It became obvious to Nasser that even if it were not the best military strategy, dispersal might be the best political solution.

On the 18th September President Nasser dismissed General Ahmed Ismail Ali from his post as Chief of Staff of the Armed Forces, Admiral Fuad Mohammed Zakri, Commander of the Navy, and over 50 other senior officers of the rank of brigadier and above, who included two rear-admirals. He was obviously not satisfied with either the army or the navy, the continued friction with the Soviet advisers and the lack of progress throughout in relation to the new weaponry that had arrived from Russia. Also included amongst those dismissed were some whose political reliability he doubted, and yet others he had been compelled to use, temporarily, as essential props in his period of retention and consolidation of his power. The official reason was 'to give young, aggressive and scientifically-minded officers positions of senior command'. While it was generally true that younger officers were promoted, there were exceptions.

One of the exceptions was Major-General Mohammed Sadek, who was promoted and appointed Chief of Staff of the Armed Forces, and who at the age of 51 was only one year younger than his predecessor. His brief was to reorganize and strengthen the Egyptian forces, especially those deployed thinly along the southern part of the country, to ensure that the Israelis could not break through into the Upper Nile Valley and the hinterland generally. General Sadek had been Director of Military Intelligence for three years, before which he had commanded both an infantry and a mechanized brigade. Commissioned in 1939, he had commanded a company in the 1948 war with Israel, had been Chief of Staff to the Egyptian armed forces in the Sinai in the 1956 fighting, and had attended a course for senior officers in Russia.

Sadek was the fourth to hold this key position since the June War, the first being, of course, General Fawzi, who had become the Minister of Defence and who still retained that portfolio; although generally considered to be lacking in political acumen, he controlled the armed forces, having been chosen for his loyalty to Nasser rather than for other qualities and capabilities. He had been succeeded by General Riad, who was killed in action and was of similar stamp, although a much better organizer. But all of them belonged to the older school used to simpler weapons. Now Nasser had appointed an officer who not only had the reputation of a good organizer, but who had a more aggressive attitude and might better appreciate and cope with the sophisticated Soviet weapons and equipment in Egypt. The new Naval Commander was Rear-Admiral Abdul Rahman, who at the age of 40 was a good example of the policy of putting young officers in positions of command. The Egyptian navy had been particularly inactive.

President Nasser was feeling more secure on the political front, and in September 1969 he dismissed Ali Sabry from the ASU, the nominal excuse for Sabry's 'resignation' being that some members of his staff had been involved in customs irregularities. Sabry himself had extremely left-wing views, and was alleged to be heading a pro-Soviet faction in Egypt, where Egyptian officers were daily returning after attending courses of instruction in the Soviet Union. At about this time there were many rumours of pro-Soviet and anti-Nasser plots, but little, if any, substantial evidence to support such suggestions. Nasser was manoeuvring for complete political mastery, and Sabry was a possible alternative leader, who might be able to muster considerable Soviet support—so he had to go. Sabry's personal feud with Editor Heikal, a Nasserite, was to his detriment, and the first news the people of Egypt had of this was when *Al Ahram* announced that Sabry had been 'disciplined and removed from the ASU'. Sabry, who was eventually put under house arrest, was replaced by Sharawi Gomaa, Minister of the Interior, as being responsible for the ASU. There were other purges in progress as well. For example, about 160 members of the judiciary were dismissed, as were the senior editorial staff on the state-run newspaper *Al Ghoumera*.

Nasser was cool towards the Soviet military mission in Egypt. He wanted it to shoulder a proportion of the blame for Egyptian losses and lack of success in the air battles and on the Canal front, and to admit that these were partly due to poor Soviet material and partly to wrong advice. But the military mission refused to provide this excuse for the armed forces. Also, Soviet policy was to press him to find a political rather than a military solution. On the 18th September he suddenly cancelled a proposed visit to the Soviet Union on the excuse of having influenza. Despite this attitude, the Soviet military mission had great influence and authority within the Egyptian armed forces, and was backed by Nasser and the general staff against complaints by Egyptian officers.

By September 1969 there were about 10,000 Russians in Egypt, of whom about 4,000 were military advisers and about 3,000 were involved in the completion of the Aswan Dam, while most of the remainder were concerned with technical and economic aid programmes. The Soviet military advisers were not too happy about the state of the Egyptian armed forces and they had a fairly low opinion of the Egyptian officer cadre as a whole.[1] Skilful propaganda and highly exaggerated accounts of Egyptian military activities had been reviving public confidence in the armed forces, whose morale began to rise, especially in June and July when their artillery barrages were causing so many Israeli casualties in the Bar-Lev Line, but after the air force's failure in its battles at the end of July it began to droop again. There was increasing disenchantment in the armed forces with the Russians, who continually urged the impatient Egyptian officers to be patient until they became more proficient. The Egyptian officers complained, for example, that Soviet trucks were under-powered and unsuitable for the extremes of temperature in the desert; when they asked for special parts to modify them, they were told to wait until 1971, which caused the Egyptians to experiment with fitting British and American engines to their trucks.

Soviet advisers held real power in that they controlled so many of the sophisticated weapons and equipment they provided, although Egyptians manned them. This was resented by the Egyptian officers, but considered essential by the Russians, and at times the situation caused friction. There had been an especially prickly incident when the Israelis raided the Egyptian coast in their ten hour war (on the 9th September). After landing at El Khafayer the Israelis attacked the SAM-2 missile base there, and the Egyptian officers demanded to be allowed to bring the missiles into action against the Israeli aircraft overhead, asking for the missile fuses, which were held by the Soviet advisers. The Russians refused on the grounds that the Egyptians were neither trained nor ready to engage such a number of Israeli planes. The Egyptians insisted, and the senior Soviet officer[2] went

---

[1] *Pravda* of the 13th September 1969.
[2] Colonel Konovalov, reputed to be the senior Soviet officer south of Port Suez.

to the top of the bunker to see for himself and was killed.[1] The Russians blamed the Egyptians for his death. Again, Nasser backed the Soviet advisers, and the local Egyptian area commander and four senior Egyptian naval officers were relieved of their duties and 'investigated'.

Clandestine leaflets were issued periodically by an underground organization known as the Free Egypt Movement (Misr al-Hurra), and one of them called for the mobilization of public opinion to prevent these five Egyptian officers being made scapegoats for the death of the Russian officer. Little was known about this Free Egypt Movement, which was said to be composed of students, workers and army officers, and whose object was to free their country from Soviet domination. Some felt it might be a 'front organization' instigated by Israeli agents, and others that it had some connexion with the illegal Muslim Brotherhood, which still had roots and sympathy in sections of the population.

There were already detachments of Algerian, Kuwaiti and Sudanese troops in the Canal Zone in the front line, but they only amounted to token gestures. Nasser wanted more practical help from the Arab states to prosecute his war of attrition, so on the 25th August 1969 the Foreign Ministers of the 14 Arab League[2] countries met in Cairo to plan an intensified combined armed effort against Israel—but it was all talk. On the 1st September 1969 King Idris of Libya, while in Turkey for medical treatment, was overthrown in a bloodless coup by a military junta which proclaimed a socialist republic. Colonel Gaddafi, Chairman of the New Revolutionary Committee of Libya, tended to be anti-Western in outlook, and so allied himself with Nasser, which in some way counter-balanced the heavy influence that Saudi Arabia held over Egypt for sheer economic reasons. When, on the 21st August, an Australian Christian[3] set

[1] Six Soviet officers were killed on one day in the heavy Israeli aerial attacks of the 20th July 1969 on missile and gun sites on the Canal front. At first this was denied by both Egyptians and Russians, but it leaked out afterwards. It was also believed that Soviet advisers (number not known) had been killed on the 9th March 1969 in the barrage that killed General Riad.

[2] On the 11th September 1969 the Arab League Council decided to extend indefinitely the term of office of its Secretary-General, Abdul Khalek Hassouna, who had held the post since its inception in 1952.

[3] Michael Rohen, who was later brought to trial, but in December 1969 was committed to a mental hospital for an undefinite period.

fire to the Aksa Mosque in Jerusalem, Nasser sought to make capital of this act to inspire a holy war against Israel, but he could raise no enthusiasm amongst Arab countries.

Meanwhile, on the 1st July, after the fifteenth session of unsuccessful talks by representatives of the Big Four[1] at the UN in New York to try to find a solution to the Middle East problem, it was announced that further meetings would be suspended during the summer. In fact, they did not meet again until the 2nd December. On the 7th July U Thant, in his report to the UN Security Council, spoke of 'open warfare' being waged along the length of the Suez Canal, and called the UN observers 'defenceless targets in a shooting gallery', threatening to withdraw them. The UN observers were composed of army officers from seven nations, who manned the 36 concrete reinforced bunkers, marked with the UN flag, for nine days at a time. The combatants had agreed not to locate weapons within 50 metres of these posts, but this rule was ignored by both sides; for example, in June the UN observers lodged 74 complaints of this nature against Egypt and 15 against Israel. Nasser wanted the UN observers to remain, as, like the former UN emergency force that had been in position on the Egyptian frontier with Israel before the June War, their presence gave him an additional excuse for not advancing into the Sinai. On the 27th July a Swedish UN observer was killed by an Israeli shell near Port Tewfik on the Egyptian side, and General Odd Bull ordered two UN observer posts on each side of the Canal to be closed down owing to the danger.

Apart from air activities, commando operations across the Canal were undertaken by both sides, especially the Egyptians, and the propaganda battle continued. On the 28th September the Egyptians claimed to have made a successful airborne raid on Israeli positions near Masfak, some 50 miles east of Kantara, claiming to have taken the Israelis by surprise, killing and wounding many and damaging vehicles and equipment. The caustic Israeli comment was that there had been no such raid, and that one Egyptian plane had dropped bombs harmlessly in the sand. As always, the truth was somewhere between the two versions.

On the 3rd October it was reported in *Al Ahram* that the battle against Israel had entered a new stage with two recent attacks by

[1] Sometimes referred to as the Big Two, meaning just America and the Soviet Union.

'specialized commando forces' on enemy positions. The same day, after a heavy artillery barrage, an 80-man commando unit, in rubber boats, crossed the Canal and stormed Israeli positions opposite Deir Suwar, in the area of the Great Bitter Lakes, but the Israelis claimed to have repulsed it with heavy casualties. Again, on the 4th, when Egyptian commandos crossed the waterway to attack Israeli positions in the Deversoir area, both sides claimed to have inflicted casualties on the other. On the 14th the Egyptians claimed to have attacked Israeli positions on the east bank and ambushed two vehicles. There was no doubt that the Egyptians made a number of commando landings on the east bank of the Suez Canal, but these were either ignored or played down by Israeli propaganda.

The Israelis also carried out commando operations, but apart from their deep penetration raids they gave them far less publicity, and on occasions they were suspected of wearing Egyptian uniforms. On the 28th October it was announced that the Israelis had carried out three commando raids inside Egypt in the past week, two being on the Gulf of Suez and the other 100 miles south-west of Sharm El Sheikh, and that six Egyptian soldiers had been wounded in them. No further details were given. The Egyptians did not comment.

On the 5th November an Egyptian commando group crossed the Canal and ambushed an Israeli patrol six miles north of Port Tewfik, near El Shatt, killing one officer and six soldiers and capturing another, who later died of wounds. This was their first daylight raid; they were getting bolder. The following day, Egyptian commandos crossed at night again just north of El Shatt when they suffered one killed and one wounded, and the same night there was another commando crossing just north of Kantara. On the 7th another Egyptian commando unit crossed the waterway and ambushed an Israeli patrol in the El Kaff sector, wounding five Israelis. This series of raids provoked Moshe Dayan to say, on the 8th, that he was working on a military reply to them.

The Egyptian navy roused itself and came into action on the night of the 8th November when two destroyers, accompanied by missile boats, approached the Sinai coast about 15 miles east of Port Said and fired shells into Israeli positions in the Romani area, until the appearance of Israeli aircraft caused them to sail away hastily. The Egyptians claimed they caused casualties and left fires blazing in fuel and ammunition dumps, but the Israelis said that the '35 minute bombardment' did no damage. On the 13th Moshe Dayan[1] decried press reports that this shelling indicated better Egyptian naval tactics, explaining that Egyptian ships could not venture any farther eastwards to bombard settled parts of the Israeli coastline as this would mean from five to six hours steaming time, which would expose them in daylight, when they would be attacked by Israeli aircraft. He commented that Israel had clearly won the last round against Egypt, but added pessimistically that the next one would be in the following spring, and optimistically that it need not necessarily be one of all-out war. Egyptian naval commandos also became active; on the 16th November five underwater explosions occurred to two Israeli ships in Eilat harbour, one of which had to be beached to save it from sinking. The Egyptians claimed it was the work of their frogmen, who had been transported there by helicopter, although more probably they had operated from adjacent Akaba, the Jordanian port.

Commando raids continued. On the 30th November the Egyptians claimed that 130 commandos crossed near El Shatt and occupied Israeli positions, remaining in them for two hours; that the Egyptian barrage kept Israeli reinforcements at a distance; and that Israeli planes later bombed their own positions, thinking the Egyptians were still in them. The Israelis said that the Egyptians had been repelled by ground fire and air support; that five Egyptians had been killed; and that the Israelis suffered neither casualties nor damage. It was continuing claim and counter-claim. On the 9th December the Egyptians claimed to have brought down their first Phantom aircraft, but this was denied by the Israelis. On the 14th President Nasser boasted of Egyptian readiness for war, saying that he had 500,000 men under arms, and that he had ordered a series of daytime commando raids across the Canal. Raids were made, but not so many in daylight, and on the 15th the Egyptians claimed to have killed an Israeli officer as well as five other occupants of a vehicle in an ambush on the east bank. On the 17th Israeli aircraft attacked the area of the southern end of the Canal for three hours, after artillery

[1] Moshe Dayan also stated that since the 1st April 1969 Egypt had made 15 commando landings, apart from naval bombardments, and that these attacks (together with air attacks) had cost the Israelis 49 casualties and the Egyptians 30 casualties. He also said that in 65 Israeli air sorties, and an undisclosed number of commando landings, the Egyptians had incurred about 1,000 casualties and the Israelis only 20, although the latter figure was later amended to 70.

fire had killed two Israeli soldiers and one civilian during the previous night.

On the 18th the Egyptians said that their commandos attacked Israeli positions, killing three soldiers and destroying tanks and vehicles, but the Israelis claimed that the Egyptians were intercepted and driven back before they reached the Israeli positions. On the 19th the Israelis claimed that one of their commando groups had penetrated Egyptian lines, through the El Ballah area, and exploded rockets at a military camp in the Salkiya area, just to the west, and that all returned safely. Playing the Israelis at their own game, the Egyptians blandly denied that there had been any such raid. And so on, and so on.

Towards the end of 1969 the morale of both the Egyptian armed forces and the nation tended to sag; most of the SAM-2 sites on the Canal Zone had been destroyed, as had many radar posts, while many new aircraft had been lost. Egyptian casualties were mounting, there was frustration at not being allowed to mount an offensive, and there was an internal refugee problem of about 500,000 people from the Canal area to cope with. The Egyptian army was bogged down in defence, both physically and mentally. Despite the adverse situation, on the 6th November President Nasser made a fiery speech, in which he declared that war with Israel was the only course left open to the Arabs, who had no alternative but to 'wage the battle of destiny against Israel . . . that this battle must be fought . . . across a sea of blood and a horizon of fire'. This did not endear him to the Soviet Government, still anxious for a political solution. Nasser's efforts to dominate and unite the Arabs under his leadership against the Israelis again met with failure at the discordant Rabat summit conference, which opened on the 19th December and broke up on the 26th without issuing a communiqué, Nasser having walked out from its final session.

Previously, on the 18th November, the Defence Minister, Mohammed Fawzi, had also made a boastful speech to the National Assembly, claiming that Egyptian soldiers had 'great fighting efficiency due to the development in training and armament', and that they were taking a monthly toll of 150 Israelis killed (which was incorrect). He said, with doubtful validity, but obviously to reassure the nation, that the Soviet Union was supplying Egypt with equipment it had not possessed before. But behind the brave façade unease

G   97

and anxiety prevailed. On the 9th December Anwar Sadat,[1] Nasser's personal representative, together with Foreign Minister Riad and Defence Minister Fawzi, flew to Moscow to try to persuade the Soviet Government that all attempts at a political solution in the Middle East were futile, and to ask for support for a more military stance by Egypt. Talks lasted for three days, and the Egyptians had some modest success. Fawzi asked for the newer MiG-21J, which would have been a match for the Israeli Phantoms, and this matter was considered.

Turning now to Israel, during the summer of 1969 morale had also tended to sag, owing to the continuing toll of casualties[2] and Nasser's perpetual talk of his war of attrition and of the coming 'battle of destiny' with Israel. Although outwardly confident, the Israeli cabinet was anxious to obtain more modern, sophisticated aircraft, expecially more Phantoms and Skyhawks. So, in September, Premier Golda Meir, accompanied by Brigadier Hod, the Israeli Air Force Commander, went to America to ask President Nixon for at least an additional 25 Phantoms and 80 Skyhawks. On the 25th, when leaving Washington, she said: 'I am leaving with a much lighter heart than when I came'.

When Richard Nixon became President of the United States in January 1969 the Russians had hoped that he would modify American policy towards the Middle East and be less inclined to provide support for Israel automatically, particularly as he had no special obligation to the American Jewish vote. Contrary to their expectations, for several months Nixon continued to follow President Johnson's policy. Then, after Premier Meir's visit to Nixon in September, warmer feelings towards Israel seemed to have been unexpectedly generated. President Nixon believed that Nasser was the only Arab leader strong and capable enough to negotiate a Middle East peace settlement, but Nasser's unyielding demand for a military solution seemed to rule out this course, and accordingly encouraged Nixon to be more generous with arms to Israel than before. The Soviet Government was also alarmed that America was allowing its citizens to enrol in the Israeli armed forces, feeling that it might be

[1] On the 20th December 1969 Nasser re-established the post of Vice-President, to which he appointed Sadat.

[2] On the 25th September 1969 Dayan stated that Israel had lost 450 killed and 1,700 wounded on all fronts since the June War.

a loophole for providing American pilots for the Phantoms sent to Israel.

Although Israeli elections were held on the 28th October 1969, it was not until the 15th December that Premier Meir was able to form a coalition government, her Labour Party not having gained a clear majority. The coalition was of five political parties, representing about 90 per cent of the electorate; Ygal Alon remained Deputy Premier, and after some hesitation Moshe Dayan agreed to join the Government, continuing as Defence Minister, which, in short, meant that Israeli policies remained as they were, with perhaps if anything a slightly more 'hawkish' outlook. The attitude hardened, and Dayan stated that time was on the side of the Israelis, who would no longer contemplate withdrawing from the occupied territories without a permanent peace settlement. He later stated, on the 6th January 1970, that in the eight months of April through to November 1969 the Israelis had lost 113 dead and 330 wounded on the Canal front, while the Egyptians must have had more than 1,000 casualties.

In October (1969) Moshe Dayan had said that the Israeli military position had improved during the previous three months along the Canal front, despite the Egyptian build-up, although it was necessary to raise the age for reservist liability from 49 to 55 years owing to the increased demand in the country for civil defence requirements. In December the defence budget of about £350 million, about 140 per cent more than it had been just before the June War, was passed, which showed that hostilities were causing a strain on Israeli economy.

The representatives of the Big Four met again on the 2nd December, in New York, their first meeting since the 1st July, and announced their readiness to achieve a settlement on the implementation of the UN November Resolution (of 1967), but in her opening speech to the Knesset Premier Meir formally rejected their suggestions. On the 9th William Rogers, the US Secretary of State, made public for the first time proposals he had privately made to the Soviet Government on the 28th October, which were based on Israeli withdrawal from the occupied territories in return for Arab assurance of a binding peace commitment. This became known as the Rogers peace initiative. Formally rejected by Israel on the 22nd

December, and by the Soviet Union on the 23rd, it received no support at all from Arab capitals.

An event of interest occurred on the 6th December 1969 with an exchange of prisoners of war across the Suez Canal at Kantara, arranged by the International Red Cross, of two Israeli pilots for 58 Egyptians. The Egyptians consisted of one pilot, five soldiers and 52 civilians, the latter including fishermen who had strayed too near Israeli positions, those seized in commando raids, and those caught trying to infiltrate through the Israeli Canal defences along traditional smugglers' routes, who may or may not have been Fedayeen.

The year ended on a triumphant note for the Israelis, who on the 27th December made a commando raid on the Egyptian Red Sea naval base at Ras Ghaleb, about 115 miles south of Suez. While there was a diversionary three-hour air raid on Egyptian Canal positions, Israeli naval commandos crossed the 18-mile wide Gulf, landed some distance away from the port, circled through the desert and approached Ras Ghaleb from the west, successfully occupying it. Immediately Israeli helicopters flew in and took away the new mobile Soviet P-12 anti-aircraft radar system for use in conjunction with SAMs. It weighed about seven tons, had a range of 200 miles, and had just been placed there to plug a gap in the Egyptian early warning system covering the Red Sea and the south-east, and so its removal left the ports of Ghurghada and Safaga open. This was the first time eyes other than Russian ones had seen this radar, which was one of the most modern Soviet systems in service, and about which little was known. The news was not released by the Israelis until the 1st January 1970, by which time, not quite knowing how the Russians might react, they had quietly returned it. The raid caught the world's imagination for its daring and initiative. The Egyptians admitted that they had lost two killed and four prisoners.

The year 1969 ended for the Israelis on an even more headline catching event that fired imagination and raised Israeli morale. They had ordered 12 250-ton gunboats from the French, which were constructed at Cherbourg, of which seven had been delivered before President de Gaulle's embargo. The last of the remaining five was launched on the 19th December, but all were impounded by the French authorities. On the 25th all five boats, manned by skeleton Israeli crews, slipped away, made for the open sea and arrived at Haifa on the last day of the year, to the cheers of the Israelis who crowded the port and sea shore to greet them.[1] These 12 gunboats, known to the Israelis as the Saar Class, were later shown to the public (on the 4th May 1970). They each carried eight Gabriel missiles, which were smaller than the Soviet Styx, having a warhead of about 338 lb and a range of about 20 miles. The missile had a self-contained guidance system that combined both infra-red (heat-seeking) with radar homing techniques.

[1] Two French generals were suspended and disciplinary action was taken against others for their suspected complicity—or neglect.

7 · Electronic War Develops

'This summer will be one of electronics by day and
infra-red by night'

PRESIDENT NASSER

We now come to the 'electronic character' of the war. While
the thunder of guns continued in all its intensity below and commandos stealthily raided across the Suez Canal, in the air the
sophisticated struggle between missiles and planes—the first in
history—began, with the two super powers, the Soviet Union and
America, fighting each other by proxy, as they battle-tested their
latest electronic developments and counters.

The Phantoms were fitted with a pod of Electronic Counter
Measures (ECMs) which enabled the pilots to have warning when
being attacked by a missile. Before long they had become familiar
with the change in 'pitch' in tracking signals that indicated a missile
was pursuing them, thus giving time for evasion and escape. Like
the American pilots in Vietnam, the Israelis called this the 'SAM
Song'. Next, America sent more pods that were able not only to
detect but also to divert oncoming missiles. The smaller and slower
(up to 675 mph) but highly manoeuvrable Skyhawks, reputed to be
one of the best all-round tactical bombers in the world, were also
fitted with ECM pods.

With this distinct advantage over the SAMs, Israeli aircraft were
able to penetrate farther into Egypt. During the first quarter of 1970
they not only knocked out the greater part of the Egyptian early
warning system along the Canal front, but they also struck at rear
Egyptian radar positions, effectively neutralizing at least three-
quarters of the country's radar protection, thus enabling the Israeli
pilots to have almost the freedom of Egyptian air space. Despite
their disadvantages, Egyptian pilots still attacked the Bar-Lev Line,
but lacking a good ground control system they were fairly ineffective
against Israeli aircraft that began to raid deeper and deeper into

Egypt in retaliation for Egyptian artillery barrages against the Bar-Lev Line.

When the Soviet Union rejected the Rogers peace initiative on the 23rd December 1969 it became clear to the Israelis that the Egyptians would not negotiate from a position of inferiority. Therefore, in the New Year, using their Phantoms, they began a phase of strategic bombing of targets in the Nile Valley, the Delta and to the west of the Canal. Moshe Dayan stated that its purpose was to prevent Egyptian preparations for a renewed offensive, to relieve pressure on the Bar-Lev Line and to convince the Egyptians that its leadership was unable to protect them. 'All Egypt is our battlefield', he boasted, adding: 'There will be no limits on military objectives within the UAR until Cairo respects the cease-fire'. Later Premier Meir said: 'We're not bombing the interior to force him (Nasser) to make peace. We go into the interior in order to make it well known to him and the people of Egypt that either it's quiet on both sides or there's bombing on both sides'.

On the 1st January 1970, in a speech to Sudanese senior officers, Nasser said that he was building an army of one million men to control Israel, and that his strategy was based on 'maintaining superiority in the air'. On the same day Colonel Gaddafi, of Libya, agreed to double his contribution to Egypt, from £30 million to £60 million, in return for help from Egyptian industrial and oil experts. On the 3rd Nasser, in an interview with *Africasia*, said that the Israeli air force 'had great superiority' and that although the Egyptian air force had as many planes, it lacked trained pilots. He claimed that in five years (i.e. 1975) Egypt would have a parity in pilots and would be able to 'crush the superiority' of the Israelis.

On the 4th January there was an aerial clash over the northern part of the Canal, the Israelis claiming two Egyptian planes and the Egyptians claiming one Israeli aircraft brought down near Kantara. The first strategic deep-penetration bombing raids began on the 7th, on three military installations, one at Inshas, about 25 miles north-east of Cairo, one at Dahsur in the Nile Valley about 32 miles south of Cairo, and the other at Tel El Kebir, 25 miles east of Cairo on the road to Ishmailia. On the 10th the Egyptians hit back, raiding Ras Sudar on the Gulf of Suez; and in the resultant air fighting they claimed to have destroyed a HAWK missile base, but the Israelis denied this and counter-claimed that they had brought down two

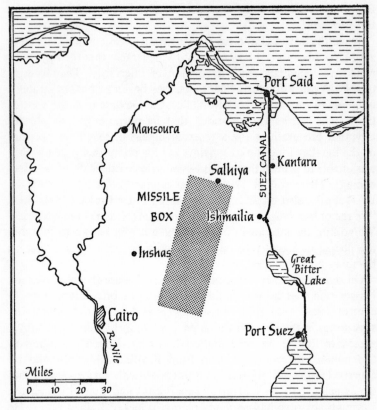

Suez Canal Zone—showing SAM box

Egyptian SU-7s that were attempting to bomb Israeli installations. On the 13th another Israeli deep penetration raid hit at the El Khanka supply depot, about 15 miles to the north-east of Cairo, this being the nearest bombing to the capital since the June War.

On the 16th the Israelis made more strategic bombing raids, mainly in the area of Tel El Kebir, losing one plane to anti-aircraft fire, which they admitted as their 16th loss since the June War (on all fronts), as against a claimed 64 Egyptian aircraft brought down by them. Also hit was an Egyptian radar position near Bir Udeib, 20 miles south of Suez. On the 18th, as well as attacking positions along the Canal front, the Israelis raided a military camp at Huckstep, about 10 miles from Cairo International airport, and also fuel and ammunition dumps at Wadi Hof, about 12 miles south-east of Cairo. The bombs were creeping closer to the capital.

On the 22nd Israeli paratroops in helicopters attacked Shadwan Island, at the entrance to the Gulf of Suez. Although the position seemed hopeless the small Egyptian garrison, whose morale was high, refused to surrender and had to be forcibly overrun by the attackers. At about the same time two Egyptian MTBs were sunk by Israeli aircraft about ten miles south of Shadwan Island. The Israelis claimed to have killed about 70 Egyptians, which number included 40 in the two MTBs, and taken 62 prisoners for the cost of three dead and six wounded. The Israelis appear to have intended to remain in occupation, knowing the Egyptians would have difficulty in ejecting them. When news of this Israeli landing reached Nasser he was reported[1] to have told the Soviet Ambassador to Egypt that he now had no option but to launch a major assault to retake it, but the Soviet Ambassador strongly advised against this course, as it would spotlight the crisis. In this instance the 'hot line' between Washington and Moscow was used, and American pressure was put on the Israelis to withdraw, which they did after 36 hours in occupation, taking with them prisoners, quantities of arms, ammunition and equipment, and a complete British Decca radar unit. Two days later at Eilat, on the 24th, 19 Israelis were killed and 41 injured when a truck, loaded with land mines captured on Shadwan Island, exploded when its wheel hit the landing ramp as it was unloading the landing-craft. Both the Egyptians and the Fedayeen claimed credit for this explosion, which was accidental.

President Nasser began to have political anxieties, feeling that if the Soviet Union failed to supply him with more sophisticated arms to match those possessed by the Israelis, he would lose the confidence of his people. Indeed, several pundits predicted that his Government would fall in the spring. On the 22nd, when the Israelis had just occupied Shadwan Island, he—despite the contrary advice given him by the Soviet Ambassador—requested an urgent meeting with Soviet leaders and later that day secretly flew to Moscow, where he remained for four days. Bargaining hard, he pointed out that his defences were completely inadequate against Israeli attacks, as Soviet missiles were no match for Israeli-piloted Phantoms with their

[1] According to John Bulloch in the *Sunday Telegraph* of the 1st February 1970.

latest ECM pods. Revealing his general lack of confidence in Soviet arms generally, Nasser requested long-range aircraft for use against Israeli urban centres in reprisal for their deep penetration raids, a policy he wanted to follow at least until his air defences had been strengthened and modernized.

The Soviet Government saw that something must be done and that Egyptain morale should be boosted, but it refused the request for long range bombers, and instead promised other forms of military aid. In a later speech (to the ASU on the 23rd July 1970) Nasser stated that the Russians promised to provide means to defend civilian and economic targets in Egypt, and that this necessary material would begin arriving within 30 days. It did eventually arrive but not quite as promptly as promised. On the 1st February the Egyptian Embassy in Moscow formally denied that President Nasser had visited the Soviet Union, after the seizure by the Israelis of Shadwan Island, to ask for more missiles and some MiG-23s.

On the 23rd January Israeli aircraft again bombed camps at Huckstep and Wadi Hof. On the 25th the Israelis said that their aircraft had attacked and disabled an Egyptian naval vessel which had run aground on a reef near Shadwan Island; it was either bringing in a new garrison or was engaged in reconnaissance for reoccupation, but the Egyptians insisted that it was merely a commercial ship. There were several heavy Israeli aerial attacks along the Canal front on the 26th. On the 28th, in their twelfth deep-penetration raid, Israeli Phantoms attacked a military camp at Maadi, almost a residential suburb, only five miles from the centre of Cairo. It was the closest attack so far, and the citizens could hear gunfire and exploding bombs. The Egyptians said that three civilians were killed, 12 wounded and 12 buildings demolished. On the same day the Israelis again raided a military camp at Dahsur, while on the 30th, for the first time since the 9th December 1969, Egyptian planes in force engaged Israeli aircraft.

Editor Heikal explained that the Israelis were pursuing a three-pronged strategy by their deep-penetration bombing, with the aims firstly of dispersing Egyptian forces, secondly of extending the battle front by some 620 miles down to the border with the Sudan, and thirdly of attempting to strike into the heart of Egypt. He summed it up accurately and neatly. On the 25th January President Nixon stated that the Americans would neither impose peace terms on the

Middle East nor negotiate for them, but were prepared 'to supply military equipment necessary to support the efforts of friendly governments, like Israel's, to defend the safety of their people'. Israel immediately requested an additional 25 Phantoms and 80 Skyhawks.

This prompted a Russian response. Premier Kosygin sent a personal note on the 3rd February to President Nixon, in which he outlined the Soviet point of view, which was that it appeared that America was guaranteeing the supremacy of Israel, that Egypt was virtually defenceless against Israeli aircraft which were attacking at will, that if the West could not restrain Israel the Soviet Union would have to supply more modern arms to Egypt, and that it was America which had begun to escalate the war by supplying Phantoms with ECM pods, which required similar ECM pods to counter them. The Russians were not anxious to send their advanced electronic equipment to Egypt, partly because they did not want to reveal their classified material to the world—which would happen if any were captured—and partly because if it were placed in inexperienced hands and shown to be ineffective (as had been the case of SAM-2s in Vietnam), their prestige and credibility would be compromised.

The Kosygin note stated that the Soviet Union would send more arms to Egypt and other Arab countries because America had sent Phantoms to the Israelis. The Soviet Union had indeed tried to block the sale of these aircraft to Israel. On the 5th President Nixon replied to the Kosygin note, denying responsibility for escalating the war, calling for an arms embargo, and warning that America might be forced to sell arms to Israel to match any increase in Soviet deliveries to Egypt. From about this time the American attitude hardened as Nixon began to insist upon negotiations and a lasting peace in the Middle East, rather than simply a political settlement as was favoured by the Russians.

On the 2nd February Egyptian planes hit at Israeli positions along the Bar-Lev Line, and returned to the attack several times during the following days. On the 5th the Israelis revealed that Soviet technicians were equipping the Egyptian MiG-21s with air-to-ground missiles and bombs. On the 8th the Israelis made more deep-penetration raids, that included camps near Tel El Kebir, at Asyut in the Nile Valley and at Helwan, the air base at Inshas, and installations at the Red Sea ports of Ghurghada and Safaga. On most days there were dog fights over the Canal; the Israelis admitted losing one plane, its pilot becoming a prisoner, but they claimed two Egyptian aircraft brought down, while the Egyptians said they had destroyed a Phantom and a Skyhawk.

On the 12th February Israeli aircraft hit a scrap metal processing plant that produced 75,000 tons of iron ingots annually, at Abu Zambal, about 15 miles north-east of Cairo, when about 2,000 workers were about to start the day shift, killing 68 of them and injuring another 98. The Israelis at once admitted that the bombing was a mistake and that the target should have been the air force supply base at El Khanka, about two miles away. Moshe Dayan immediately warned that the aircraft had dropped a delayed action bomb that was due to explode in 24 hours. It was later stated that the Israeli pilot's radar operated bomb-site had failed and the pilot had to seek his target visually, being some two miles out in his calculations. The Egyptians claimed that the Israelis had dropped napalm, which Dayan denied. President Nasser later (on the 18th March) stated that his advisers had wanted him to authorize Egyptian deep-penetration raids, but that he had refused; and he then again repeated that although the Egyptian and Israeli air forces had about the same number of planes, the Israelis were three times stronger in effect as they had three times as many pilots. Also, on the 12th, Israeli aircraft struck at a radar position at Jebel Aweibid, about 25 miles west of the Canal. After the Abu Zambal error, the Israelis suspended their strategic bombing raids for three days.

On the 14th a total blackout was ordered in Cairo and other cities, as the Abu Zambal raid brought the war dramatically and forcibly home to the Egyptians. On the 15th, in an interview,[1] President Nasser said that he would be pressing the Russians to supply him with MiG-23s and the latest electronic equipment to counter Israeli aircraft; he was hesitating to ask for Soviet pilots but he might do this if the Israelis carried on with their offensive against Egyptian industrial centres. On the 16th the Soviet news agency, Tass, announced that the Soviet Union would provide the 'necessary support' to the Arab countries to ensure their security against Israeli attacks, to which, on the 17th, the US State Department in Washington reiterated that its intention was to make arms available to the Israelis to maintain a military balance in the Middle

[1] With James Reston of the *New York Times*.

East. In the Knesset Premier Meir said that if the Egyptians would respect the cease-fire Israel would do the same, otherwise Israel would 'strike close to home'.

The Israeli strategic bombing raids, which were designed to bring home to the people of Egypt the consequences of Nasser's war of attrition, had the rather contrary effect of making Nasser more popular with the masses than ever before, as they were appalled at the killing of innocent non-combatants. A resultant demand grew for pressure on America to cease supplying planes to Israel, and for the Soviet Union to be urged to provide more modern aircraft and electronic equipment to Egypt.

President Nasser said that Israel could have peace only after it had evacuated all the occupied territories, including Jerusalem, readmitted the Palestinian refugees and established a multi-racial instead of a Jewish state, when Arab recognition of Israel and freedom of navigation on the Suez Canal would follow. On the 18th, in his report to Congress on foreign policy, President Nixon warned that attempts to establish Soviet domination in the Middle East would be a matter of grave concern. On the 20th the Soviet Ambassador to the UN rejected proposals by America, Britain and France for Middle East settlements, and also the American proposal to start talks on arms limitations to the Middle East. The Soviet Union feared that the Israelis were deliberately trying to bring Nasser down because of his rigid attitude towards a peace settlement, and that America was supporting Israel in this attempt.

Israeli deep-penetration raids were resumed on the 14th, on which day the Israelis brought down an Egyptian SU-7 by anti-aircraft fire over the Canal, claiming it to be the 68th since the June War. On succeeding days other raids against radar positions, missile sites and military installations followed. On the 19th, when Egyptians bombed Israeli positions on the east bank of the Canal near Kantara and near the Great Bitter Lakes, an Israeli plane was shot down, being admitted as the 19th since the June War on all fronts. On the following day the Egyptians claimed their score to have been 140 Israeli aircraft, including two in 'the last 24 hours'. On the 25th the Canadian Broadcasting Corporation stated that the Israelis were receiving four Phantoms a month to complete the original order of 50 by June 1970, and that America had agreed to provide an additional 25 if there were no halt in the arms race.

On the 26th the Israelis raided a SAM base only three miles south-west of Cairo, and other targets in the Delta, and when Egyptian planes scrambled to intercept them a number of dog fights broke out. The Israelis claimed to have shot down three Egyptian MiGs by cannon fire when attacking a missile site at Dukhmeis, about 70 miles north of Cairo.

The struggle in the air continued on into March, there seldom being a day without dog fights over the Canal area and Israeli aerial assaults. On the 1st, for example, the Egyptians claimed that 32 soldiers and civilians were killed by Israeli air raids. On the 6th March, when the Israelis struck at a radar position near Damietta, they claimed to have shot down two MiGs that attacked them. On the 12th Israeli aircraft hit radar sites at Abu Suweir, eight miles west of Ishmailia, and also at Jebel Aweibid on the Cairo road again, on which day the Israelis said that they shot down an Egyptian SU-7 over the Sinai—which showed that Egyptian pilots penetrated Israeli air space. On the following day the Egyptians stated that five civilians had been killed and 36 injured by delayed action bombs in a raid on the village of Sarsak, near Mansoura.

Suddenly, on the 18th March, US sources announced that the Soviet Union had begun the delivery in large numbers of SAM-3s to Egypt. On the next day the *New York Times* reported that at least 1,500 Soviet personnel—about 1,000 technicians and 500 soldiers to guard them—had arrived in Egypt with the SAM-3s. Almost all the SAM-2 sites along the Canal front and elsewhere in Egypt had been eliminated, and although more were constantly being established in their place, the American ECM pods enabled low-flying Israeli pilots to dodge the missiles almost effortlessly, the SAM-2 not being very effective below 2,000 feet. Within days the Israelis had located up to 15 SAM-3 sites around Cairo, Alexandria, the Aswan Dam and certain airfields. Many more SAM-2s were arriving and were being formed into a SAM box. Radar-controlled anti-aircraft guns were also being delivered.

First seen in Soviet service in 1964, the SAM-3, installed on Soviet warships, was also a high altitude weapon, with a 'slant range' of about 33 miles and an upper ceiling of about 40,000 feet, its lower one not being known. It had advanced radar and electronic equipment, which was less vulnerable to jamming than that of the SAM-2. The SAM-3 was on a mobile launcher, but had to stop to fire the missile, which was a two-stage, solid fuel one, about 18 feet long. Considered superior to the American HAWK, it also had the inherent problem of target identification.

Under Russian supervision and guidance, the Egyptians worked on constructing a solid defensive belt about 16 miles wide and over 50 miles long parallel to the Canal and between 20–30 miles from it on its western side, in which SAM-2s and anti-aircraft guns were linked to radar posts. To form a complete barrier against Israeli aerial attack meant positioning several batteries of SAMs fairly close together so that their trajectories interlocked and saturated air space in front of them. A strong SAM box was something the Israelis feared, as it would restrict their movement in the air; accordingly, during the last ten days or so of March the Israeli air force, in furious strength, attempted to destroy it, some raids lasting up to four hours at a time. Although many SAM sites were knocked out, more SAMs were brought in. Despite this intense Israeli pressure, the SAM box took shape, but it was not a barrier as long as the Israeli pilots had ECM pods that enabled them to avoid the missiles. At the same time other deep-penetration raids were made and radar positions were especially attacked. Egyptian aircraft scrambled frequently to meet Israeli attackers; on the 27th, for example, the Israelis claimed five MiGs in a battle north of Suez, three being shot down, one exploding in mid-air and the other crashing, which brought the Israeli claimed total up to 85, for the admitted loss of 11 of their own on this front. On the last day of March the Egyptians said that 12 civilians had been killed and 35 injured at Mansoura in an Israeli air raid.

While all this activity was going on overhead, the artillery on both sides of the Canal continued shelling almost endlessly, and there was intermittent commando activity as well. The Egyptians had about 15 tough and well trained units of 'special troops', while the Israelis used naval commandos, of which they had about 500, or their paratroops, for this purpose. On the 5th February Egyptian frogmen entered Eilat harbour and caused underwater explosions to two small ships; one sank and the other had to be beached to save it from sinking. The following day, in reprisal, Israeli aircraft sank a Soviet built Egyptian minelayer, near Ghurghada in the Red Sea, but there was no loss of life. Also, on the 5th, Egyptian commandos crossed the Canal near El Cap, about 20 miles south of Port Said, and claimed to have destroyed two Israeli tanks, two armoured vehicles and a jeep in ambush. On the 7th General Bar-Lev admitted that the Eilat action and 'some Canal crossings' were Egyptian successes, and he spoke of a 'few hundred well trained combative Egyptian soldiers'. That the problem was admitted by the Israelis showed how much it hurt.

On the 11th February the Egyptians said that a commando unit crossed the Canal and caused 20 Israeli casualties, but the Israelis denied this, commenting that only three of their soldiers had been wounded that day by shell fire. Previously, on the 27th January, when the Egyptians had claimed that their commandos had penetrated through the Sinai and raided Israeli positions at Gaza, the Israelis denied there had been any such raid. The war of communiqués was still waged fiercely.

On the 14th March the Israelis, crossing the waterway in rubber boats, made a frontal assault in daylight against four Egyptian positions, which they occupied for a short while, at the cost of two killed and four wounded; they claimed to have killed eight Egyptians. Some buildings were demolished. The Israelis asserted that the operation had proved Israeli ability to establish a bridgehead on the west bank, but the Egyptians claimed that the raid was foiled by their gunners, who sank several boats and so prevented a landing. On the 22nd two Israelis were killed and 11 injured when two trucks hit a land mine about 50 miles south of El Arish, which showed that either Egyptian commandos or Fedayeen roamed parts of the Sinai desert despite Israeli denials. On the 26th Egyptian commandos crossed the Canal near the northern end in daylight to ambush an Israeli patrol, killing one officer and wounding three soldiers. And so on.

Turning to the political scene, it was reported that on the 15th March 1970 Colonel Gaddafi withdrew his 800-strong Libyan detachment from the Canal Zone. Originally sent by King Idris, it had been there since June 1967. In fact, the move was merely a political change-over of personnel and fresh Libyan soldiers were sent in their place. Next, in the hope that it might generate some good will on the part of Russia, on the 23rd US Secretary of State William Rogers announced that President Nixon had decided to hold in abeyance the Israeli request for the extra 25 Phantoms and 80 Skyhawks, which brought no reciprocal response. On the contrary, three days later, on the 26th, it was reported that the Soviet Mediterranean Fleet had been reinforced by two new Soviet helicopter-carriers, which brought its number of craft up to 50, and included about 13 submarines.

Israeli strategic air strikes continued. On the 8th April the Egyptians claimed that the Israelis had bombed a school in the village of Bahr El-Bakr, about 20 miles west of Kantara. First reports stated that 30 children had been killed and more than 50 injured, but the figures were later amended to 46 killed, some of the injured having later died. On the following day journalists were shown the bodies, but were not allowed to see the actual building, which the Israelis claimed was used for military purposes. Moshe Dayan showed photographs of a fortress-like building with military vehicles in the courtyard, and said that if part of it was used as a school it showed 'criminal irresponsibility'. On the 15th an Israeli spokesman said they had 'irrefutable evidence' that the Egyptians had spent five days removing all traces of military occupation from the building. On the 13th Israeli strategic bombing raids were resumed, aircraft striking at targets in the Helwan area that day.

In mid-April Joseph Sisco, US Assistant Secretary of State, visited the Middle East. On the 14th he remarked on 'considerable differences of viewpoint' between Egypt and Israel, and the following day Moshe Dayan spoke out about the Russian and American attitudes, saying that Israel might have to fight on alone for survival if abandoned by the West. He said that the Russians had now become a major military problem for the Israelis, for unless they manned only the SAM-3s, which were not essential targets for Israeli defence, a clash could not be avoided. He was obviously referring to the possibility of Soviet pilots being used against the Israelis, and added: 'We shall have to, and I hope we will, achieve a co-existence with the Russians in the skies of Egypt—not in the skies of Israel'—but his hope was wildly over-optimistic.

When President Nasser had asked for MiG-23s from the Russians he had argued that if he did not obtain them he would either have to send up his inexperienced pilots against the Israeli aircraft, which would have meant disastrous losses, or sit and watch his SAM box being destroyed, although it was not specifically mentioned who would pilot them. The Soviet answer had been in two parts, the first being the dispatch of the SAM-3s, which had arrived in March, to guard certain cities, airfields and the Aswan Dam. By the middle of April over 20 batteries, manned by Soviet personnel, were deployed within Egypt, which progressively restricted Israeli freedom of Egyptian air space. The Israelis could not risk causing Soviet casualties deliberately as they did not know exactly how the Soviet Government would react. The second part was the dispatch of new Soviet MiG-21Js which, together with Soviet pilots and ground crews, began to arrive in Egypt in early April, and were deployed to special air bases entirely under Soviet control. The MiG-21J was an improved MiG-21; it had better radar, more effective fire control, and it could carry extra wing-tip fuel tanks, which gave it sufficient range to strike into Israel. The Soviet piloted MiG-21Js soon numbered about 150. By mid-April they had assumed responsibility for the defence of the Nile Valley and the Delta, which abruptly brought the Israeli phase of strategic deep-penetration bombing to an end, the last raid being carried out on the 17th April. Thus, by this adroit move, the extremely valuable option had been suddenly whisked away from the Israeli air force. Brigadier Hod, Commander of the Israeli air force, later described the situation as 'a Russian fist covered by an Egyptian glove'. It meant that Moshe Dayan was no longer able to boast, as he had done earlier in January, that 'all Egypt is our battlefield'.

8 · The Electronic Battle

'This summer is going to be an electrifying one—an electronic one'
MOSHE DAYAN

Once it became obvious that Soviet pilots had assumed responsibility for the air defence of the Nile Valley and the Delta, and that Soviet personnel were manning SAM-3 batteries, Israeli strategic deep penetration raids had to cease. Egyptian pilots were thus released for deployment in the Canal Zone, and the focus of the air force was turned against the Bar-Lev Line. On the ground, artillery activity increased also, and some 27 Israelis were killed in April. Over 200 Soviet pilots had been flying on training missions over Egypt for over two years, but this was a different matter.

From the 19th to the 21st April Egyptian fighter planes struck almost continuously at east bank positions, and in the fighting the Israelis claimed two Egyptian aircraft. On the 23rd Egyptian planes penetrated the Sinai to attack Nahal Yam, an Israeli military settlement, but the Israelis said that there were no casualties. On the following day, in retaliation, Israeli aircraft in strength assaulted west bank positions. A heavy artillery barrage occurred on the 28th, the Israelis stating that the Egyptians fired over 1,000 shells within 24 hours. Both on the 28th and the 29th there was much aerial activity by both sides over the Canal, the Israelis claiming to have brought down two SU-7s over the Sinai.

President Nasser said on the 21st April that Israeli air raids only cemented Egyptian national unity and their determination to go on fighting until victory, adding: 'We have completely rebuilt our defensive strength, and we are capable of answering Israeli aggressions with large-scale counter-offensives'. On the 26th Mohammed Hassanein Heikal, Editor of *Al Ahram*, was appointed Minister of National Guidance, part of his new job being to control the Egyptian television, press and information services, including the Middle

East News Agency. He retained his editorship, and his predecessor, Mohammed Fayek, became Foreign Minister.

At the same time commando raiding across the waterway continued. The Egyptians, on the 26th, claimed to have made two forays. One, they claimed, was made by 200 men at El Shatt, in the southern sector, who 'wiped out 35 Israelis' as well as destroying tanks and trucks, for the loss of only 'a few Egyptian soldiers'. The Israelis issued a denial, but admitted that five of their soldiers had been wounded when a motorized patrol was ambushed. The other raid was made near El Ballah, but the Israelis claimed to have sunk several boats, each containing eight Egyptians.

On the 29th April the Egyptians stated that 600 troops had crossed the Canal on a 15-mile-wide front between El Ballah and Ishmailia, and that when they withdrew after a 12-hour battle they had killed and wounded 'tens' of Israelis and destroyed nine tanks and vehicles, for the loss of only three Egyptians killed and wounded. They claimed that this was their second major strike within a week, and that the Israelis had to call up armour to beat them back. On the other hand, the Israelis said that only about 40–50 Egyptians crossed the Canal to attack a single Israeli position, but were repulsed by air and ground forces, when four rubber boats, each containing eight soldiers, were sunk, and afterwards about 46 bodies were seen floating on the Canal. On the 3rd May Egyptian commandos crossed the Gulf of Suez and fired Katushya rockets, from a June War wreck some 800 yards off-shore from El Tor, into an Israeli camp, but the Israelis said that no casualties were caused. Certainly during the second half of April the Egyptian army was fighting with greater confidence.

An Israeli Government communiqué, issued on the 29th April, stated that Soviet pilots were carrying out operational flights from Egyptian bases, but on their missions they had not yet reached the Canal Zone, nor had they yet been engaged in battle with Israeli pilots. A military spokesman said that scores of Soviet pilots in MiG-21s were patrolling a specific area on interception operations against Israeli planes. He also estimated that the Egyptians had between 800–900 guns and 700 tanks along the Canal. Previously, on the 6th, General Bar-Lev had said that Soviet pilots formed the final link in the SAM-3 anti-aircraft defence system, and that the renewed aggressiveness of the Egyptians along the Canal had been made possible by the part played by the Russians in the skies over Egypt. He announced his intention to hit SAM-3s, despite their Russian crews, but indicated that Israeli pilots would be careful not to strike at either Port Said or Alexandria, where there were Russian ships. General Bar-Lev explained how Egyptian pilots were now using Soviet bombing techniques, coming in low against Canal positions, and then just before they reached the target suddenly pulling up to 1,500–2,000 feet to gain sufficient height to dive-bomb and then fly quickly away—in short, the same tactics as used by the Israelis in their pre-emptive strike in June 1967.

Nasser's speech at Helwan on the 1st May marked the re-emergence of a confident leader who had persuaded the Soviet Government to support his Middle East policies. He said: 'A change has taken place. Our armed forces have regained the initiative with bold military operations in the air and on land'. He added that Egyptian planes might hit Israeli civilian targets, and remarked: 'Without Soviet aid Mussa Dayan would be sitting in Cairo'. Now in a much stronger domestic position, Nasser was able to assert himself against the Fedayeen challenge, and Egyptians became more involved in strategic and operational planning. On the 4th Nasser had admitted that the Israeli strategic deep-penetration raids had wrested the military initiative from him and compelled his army to disperse into a scattered defensive posture. But the Israelis were deeply worried about what they termed 'creeping Russian aggression' and wondered exactly how far the Russians would go. Already the war had been abruptly pushed back from the Nile Valley and the Delta, and the Israelis were confined to within 25 miles of the Canal. Dayan predicted an 'electronic summer', when jets loaded with sophisticated electronic counter-measures would be matched against Soviet SAM-2s and SAM-3s.

At the beginning of May there was a renewed air of confidence in Egypt, and the lights of Cairo and other cities came on again. Throughout the month work continued on the SAM box, about 25 miles from the Canal. By mid-May the Soviet pilots were organized into 24 operational squadrons, based on four airfields near Cairo, and one at Beni Suef, about 60 miles south of Cairo. They became part of the defensive system of Egypt proper, linked in with the 20 SAM-3 batteries, each having 50 Soviet troops to guard them. So far there were no SAM-3s in the SAM box. On the 9th Moshe

Dayan said that the Soviet pilots and SAM-3s had created a critical situation, and repeated again that Israel must seek co-existence with the Russians in the skies over Egypt, indicating that he seemed resigned to accepting the 25-mile limit from the Canal, which the Russians appeared to be tacitly allowing the Israelis. On the 19th it was announced that 43 per cent of the national budget of Egypt was devoted to defence, amounting to about £553 million (afterwards formally approved on the 9th June), and on the 21st Nasser, in an interview with *Die Welt*, said: 'Soviet pilots flying for the Egyptian air force could have been in dog fights with Israeli aircraft', but it was not thought that this had happened yet. On the following day Abba Eban, Israeli Foreign Minister, in an interview with President Nixon, asked for more aircraft, but he was told that no decision had been taken.

Early in May, on the 4th, Egyptian planes raided the outskirts of El Arish, in north-eastern Sinai, when the Israelis claimed to have shot down two Il-28s, but the Egyptians would admit to the loss of only one. In the first part of the month the Israelis had been pre-occupied with their Lebanese frontier. It was not until the 14th that Israeli aerial assaults recommenced in the Canal Zone, and for a couple of days the Israelis seemed to meet with little opposition, being able to carry out attacks against concrete emplacements along the Canal for up to five hours at a time. Gradually Egyptian aircraft intervened and there were several air battles in the space between the Canal and the SAM box, the Egyptians claiming on the 16th to have shot down two Israeli aircraft, while in two days the Israelis claimed five planes, four being shot down and one, a MiG-21, exploding in mid-air. On the 19th Israeli raids were turned from the forward Canal defences on to the SAM box area to prevent reconstruction. On the 31st May the Israelis stated that since the June War 543 soldiers and 116 civilians had been killed and 1,763 soldiers and 629 civilians wounded; that during May on the ground in the Canal Zone they lost 42 soldiers killed and 106 wounded—which indicated the intensity of the fighting.

Both sides visibly flexed their muscles slightly. On the 5th May Israel put on show to the press a display of new military equipment that included two of the French-built gunboats equipped with Gabriel missiles, a 90mm anti-tank gun mounted on a half-track (M-3), capable of traversing, and a converted Patton tank, up-gunned with a 105mm gun, and powered by a US diesel engine, that gave ten running hours without refuelling, which was claimed to equal the Soviet T-55. On the other side of the waterway, during the same week, Russians watched Egyptian manoeuvres, in which an Egyptian armoured formation made assaults across water obstacles, on the lake near El Faiyum, south of Cairo, when Soviet observers were reported to have been impressed.

On the 26th May Premier Meir emphasized to the Knesset that Israel had accepted the November Resolution. It was assumed, she said, that the Soviet Union wanted frontier clashes and continued tension between Arabs and the Israelis, but not all-out war. She confirmed the estimates of 20 SAM-3 bases in the heart of Egypt, and that since the June War the Soviet Union had supplied Egypt with 650 tanks and 260 aircraft.

On the 24th May Colonel Gaddafi of Libya and President Nasser met President Numeiry in Khartoum, on the first anniversary of the coup there, to work out a common policy against Israel and agreement on increased contributions by Arab states. On the 28th, as the conference dispersed, Nasser said it was thanks to the Russians that the Israelis had been forced to stop their deep-penetration raids over Egypt. Now he was ready, he announced, to try to reach a political solution (something he had not said for months) and he affirmed that the Russians would remain in the Middle East until the Israelis evacuated the occupied territories.

During May there was activity at sea. On the 13th a 70-ton Israeli fishing boat was sunk by missiles fired from Egyptian missile boats, about 11 miles from the north Sinai coast, only two of the four crew surviving. On the 16th an Egyptian destroyer and a missile boat of the Komar Class were sunk near Ras Banas in the Red Sea by Israeli planes, which had to fly some 650 miles and return. The Egyptians confirmed the loss of these two ships, and the Israelis said that their action was in retaliation for the sinking of the fishing boat, and also for the death of an Israeli killed, while working in a wreck in Eilat harbour, by explosives placed there by Egyptian frogmen.

An interesting but little appreciated fact was that although the Israelis were extracting millions of barrels of oil from former Egyptian oil wells in the Gulf of Suez, the Egyptians did not attempt to bomb them, for the simple reason that they also had more vulnerable oil wells just to the south and on the west side of the Gulf.

It was a case of live and let live. It was also interesting to note that Israeli and Egyptian ships passed each other in the Gulf of Suez with unconcern.

Commandos were also active. On the 19th May the Egyptians stated that a force of 90 men crossed the Canal and attacked an Israeli unit near Shalloufa, in the southern sector, inflicting heavy casualties and destroying three armoured vehicles. According to the Israelis, the party numbered only 15 men, and was driven back after a three-hour engagement in which the Egyptians lost seven killed, for no Israeli loss. The Egyptians claimed that their biggest commando success occurred on the 30th, when they carried out two daylight raids. One ambushed an Israeli convoy about seven miles south of Port Fuad, causing 'dozens' of Israeli casualties and destroying several military vehicles. The Israelis admitted 15 soldiers killed, eight wounded and two missing. The other raid took place in the central sector, and there were also conflicting claims. *Al Ahram* claimed that this 'heralded a new stage in the confrontation with Israel'.

The reconstruction of the SAM box to provide relief for the battered front line positions during June had largely been an Egyptian undertaking, but it had made little progress, providing only light and ineffectual opposition to attacking Israeli aircraft. Most reports indicated the SAM batteries to be placed at intervals of 10 kilometres (about 6·2 miles) to give overlap. During the latter part of May the Russians asserted closer supervision, and also brought in a few of their own integral batteries to stiffen up the defences.

The Israelis estimated that by the 1st June about 250 Soviet pilots were flying MiG-21Js over Egypt, all the aircraft being housed in individual concrete hangars. As the Russians denied flying over Egypt they were under no obligation to admit clashes or casualties, and the Americans and Israelis were at a disadvantage as the Soviet personnel were in defensive roles, the SAMs certainly being generally regarded as defensive weapons. An additional five batteries of SAM-3s had been located, bringing the total up to 25, there still being none in the SAM box or the Canal Zone; the reason was, it was later revealed, that the Russians were having difficulty in calibrating them properly, having never fired them before under active service conditions. The Israelis had the advantage that SAM-3s and

SAM-2s could be detected by electronic reconnaissance. Normally the SAM-3s were housed in two low rectangular 40-feet long buildings that held the missiles, computers, radar and other necessary electronic equipment. One type of radar system needed a 65-feet high tower, hence the current stories that they were disguised as mosques.

The Israelis tried one or two tentative probes in the air towards the Nile Valley, but each time Soviet fighters took off to intercept them and the Israelis withdrew. Egyptian air space beyond the 25-mile limit from the Canal was effectively barred to them, so instead they hammered away at the concrete emplacements being constructed in the SAM box, as they knew that if sufficient were activated they would deprive the Bar-Lev Line, which was almost within their 'slant range', of overhead cover and so render it more vulnerable to amphibious assault. Since the 18th April the Israeli aircraft had also been concentrating heavily upon the Egyptian forward positions, and by the beginning of June the Egyptians had considerably reduced the numbers of soldiers in the Canal Zone. However, their guns remained active, but the more the Egyptian artillery shelled, the more the Israeli air force bombed.

In the air battle over the Canal on the 3rd the Israelis claimed three MiGs without loss to themselves; Egypt admitted losing one plane, but claimed two Mirages and to have hit a third. On the 5th another UN observer post was abandoned, leaving only 11 out of the original 18 on the Egyptian side. On the 9th a group of Israeli planes raided El Qassassin, which was just over 25 miles from the Canal, and on the western edge of the SAM box. This was the farthest from the Canal the Israelis had raided since mid-April. Despite many raids on the SAM box, Israeli pilots reported that the Egyptians were still building sites and shelters as fast as they were demolished.

The Israelis made a concentrated effort against Port Said. Starting on the 28th May, in eight days they carried out 100 hours of solid bombing, dropping, so the Israelis say, in that period about 4,200 bombs. By the 4th June Port Said was running short of food and water, and having to be supplied by boat, as the narrow 150-yard wide neck of land that connected the city to the mainland was so heavily cratered that transport could not pass along it. The reason for this offensive was that the Israelis thought amphibious equipment and troops might concentrate at Port Said to make a bridgehead on the eastern side of the Canal, where Israeli defences were weakest. Mohammed Fawzi, the Defence Minister, had just boasted that Egyptian troops were preparing for a big battle against the Israelis. On the 12th June a small Israeli force of commandos crossed the Canal north of Kantara, and blew up a two-mile-long stretch of fortifications that had been under aerial attack since the 28th May, it being expected that this area was to be the actual springboard for an Egyptian assault. The Israelis claimed to have killed 50 Egyptians for the loss of four killed and 15 wounded.

There were extensive marshlands on both sides of the Canal north of Kantara and in places there were adjacent lakes only separated by narrow strips of land. The most suitable terrain to make a crossing was the 20-mile stretch between Kantara and Ishmailia where the Israeli defences were naturally stronger, or perhaps 20 miles north of Kantara where the Israelis only lightly held ground because of the marsh, but both in differing ways presented great problems to the Egyptians when thinking in terms of large scale assault landings.

On the 14th President Nasser said that the confrontation on the Canal was 'real warfare', and that after the war of attrition the battle of liberation would begin, in which he hoped the whole Arab nation would join. On the following day General Bar-Lev stated that Israeli policy was no longer based on retaliation, but on continuous activity 'countering war with war'. To test Soviet reaction, on the 23rd June a small Israeli commando raid in helicopters was made against a camp at Bir Araida, when rockets were fired. Bir Araida, some 50 miles inland from the Gulf of Suez and 50 miles south of Cairo, was close to the Soviet-controlled air base of Beni Suef. The raid was not repeated.

On the 25th June 1970 US Secretary of State William Rogers announced an American initiative for peace in the Middle East, but declined to give details or discuss further support for the Israelis. He said the object was 'to stop shooting and start talking'. On the 29th Premier Meir warned against the danger of a short-term cease fire. That day, the 29th, Nasser flew to Moscow, where he was met by President Podgorny and Premier Kosygin, who said they favoured a Middle East settlement on the basis of the November Resolution.

The 30th June 1970 was a fateful day for the Israelis, partly because in aerial combat they brought down four MiG-21s, believed to be piloted by Russians (the matter was hushed up by both sides for some time) but mainly because the Israelis suddenly lost three air-craft over the Canal Zone. Two Phantoms and one Skyhawk were brought down, one by anti-aircraft fire alone and the other two by missiles. Another Phantom was brought down by a SAM-2 a few days later. The Israeli pilots had assumed their ECM pods would divert the oncoming missiles as they had done so far, but this time they did not, and the pilots were unable to take evasive action in time. They were brought down by the newer type of SAM-2, which had a 'terminal guidance radar' (that guided the missiles on to the target) possessing a greater range of frequencies, which could not be picked up by the ECM pods. Although there were rumour and speculation, the Egyptians so far still had no SAM-3s within 25 miles of the Canal. The Egyptians had gained a distinct advantage, and the thwarted Israelis had to hold off for a while until the Americans supplied them with a more up-to-date counter.

America was at the time developing a family of miniaturized high-performance electronic systems, and about 100 of the latest ECM pods, containing a greater range of frequencies and extra sensors, were sent to the Israelis within a few days. These ECM pods, carried on the wing-tips of the Phantoms, contained 'jammers' that radiated electro-magnetic waves on the same frequency used by the acquisition, tracking and guidance systems (the radar that locked on to a plane and plotted its position) on an oncoming missile. When the ECM pod was switched on, the 'jammer' disrupted the missile's frequency, causing it to veer away off-course. The improved SAM-2s had more frequencies than the first batch of ECM pods used by the Israelis, but the latest pods had many more. A counter used to avoid the effects of 'jamming' of missiles was that radio frequencies, emitted from ground control to the missile radar guidance system, could be changed quickly, so the missile radar system could continue to track the target aircraft in spite of 'jamming'. New sensors in the ECM pod enabled the pilot to detect this switch instantly; he in turn could, by a frequency shift of his own, resume 'jamming' the missile. Soon pilots and ground control staff were fully involved in the deadly game of 'jamming', 'counter-jamming', and split-second avoidance by frequency switches. Israeli Stratocruisers, packed full with electronic equipment, hovered in the background whenever Israeli aircraft moved into action. Later, when one such Stratocruiser was shot down, President Nasser gleefully described it as a 'fat catch'. The electronic war which he dreaded so much, as he feared that the Americans might outsmart the Russians in this sphere, began in earnest.

Daily, Israeli planes raided the SAM box, when SAM-2 missiles were fired at the attackers in 'ripples' or 'small waves', thus making it more difficult for aircraft to take evasive action; but by low-flying and electronic skill they lost few aircraft. The sequence of the attacks was that the Egyptians waited for Israeli aircraft to assault, when missiles were promptly fired, and then anti-aircraft guns opened up as the attacking planes came in low. Egyptian aircraft were held back, usually high overhead, ready to swoop down and engage Israeli aircraft when they were about to return home; at this stage all Egyptian missile and anti-aircraft fire momentarily ceased. Boosted by the arrival from a year's training in the Soviet Union of about 200 pilots, who were anxious to show their worth, the Egyptian air force began to demonstrate a new aggressive spirit. Showing more skill in dog fights, the Egyptians lost far fewer planes than ever before in this form of combat with the Israelis.

The Israelis tried desperately hard to eliminate the SAM box. Although they destroyed many sites, more appeared to take their place. Indeed, despite bombardments and attacks of napalm, rockets and cannon fire, the Egyptians doggedly continued working in the forward area and the SAM box at construction and repair. The Russians developed a mobile platform for the missile launchers, which enabled them to be quickly moved from position to position, or taken from prepared sites and hidden in sand hills. The Egyptians also took to moving SAM-2s forward overnight and setting them up, without any prior preparation, to surprise the Israelis in their daily dawn assaults—their speciality, as the sun rising in the east tended to blind the Egyptians facing in that direction. These clandestine moves were usually, but not always, discovered in time by the infra-red detection devices during Israeli night reconnaissance flights.

General Bar-Lev confirmed the recent losses of Israeli aircraft at a press conference on the 6th July. He said that overnight, on the 29th/30th June, a new missile system had been set up, consisting of a dozen batteries of SAM-2s, with supporting radar-controlled anti-aircraft guns, in a 'belt' (or box) about 45 miles long. He asserted that Russian planning, direction and execution were evident. The two Israeli Phantoms had been spotted and ambushed just after dawn. He also said that the battle for the west bank of the Canal had opened on the 1st July. During the next few days, the SAM box had been consolidated into a strip about 17 miles deep, with its centre on the Cairo-Ishmailia road. Dayan also spoke of the new SAM-2, saying that it had a faster computer and better flight characteristics against low altitude planes and their manoeuvrability. He also told of the new tactic of 'ripple' firing, when an entire battery of six missiles was launched in short, integrated timed sequence, making evasive action by the pilot more difficult. In North Vietnam the SAM-2s usually fired either single missiles or in salvos; the attrition rate against US aircraft was only one in 1,000 sorties. The Egyptians had fired hundreds of missiles, but until the 30th June had only succeeded in bringing down one Israeli Piper Cub.

On the 29th June President Nasser had flown to the Soviet Union, where he stayed for nearly three weeks. On the 1st July President Nixon declared that the situation in the Middle East was more dangerous than in South East Asia, because there was the possibility of a 'super power confrontation'; to avoid war it would be necessary to maintain the balance between Israel and the Arab states, so America would see that that balance was kept. But the pressure on Egypt was heavy as the Israeli air force had been pounding the Egyptian guns and their logistic support daily, and Egyptian morale was falling. It was semi-officially admitted that Egyptian casualties along the Canal during the month of June amounted to between 1,500 and 2,000.

On the 19th July, their 59th consecutive day of assaulting the SAM box, the Israelis admitted the loss of another Phantom by missile fire, but the following day they claimed four MiG–21s. Despite the incessant pounding, destroyed and damaged missile and radar sites became operational again overnight, or were dispersed to alternative locations. There seemed to be an inexhaustible supply of missiles, launchers, radars and support facilities, and it was thought to be a matter of Soviet pride to prove their weapons against Israeli aircraft. There was constant speculation about how many Russians were actually with the SAM batteries, stiffening and directing, as there was continual use of 'ripple' tactics. In short, the Israelis were unable to neutralize the SAM box, and this desperate struggle, involving so much sophisticated weaponry and counters, continued until the end of July and on into the first week of August, hardly without pause. It should be noted that the Israelis also seemed amply supplied with ammunition and ECM pods. With Soviet pilots in the background and an almost indestructible SAM screen, it appeared that the Israeli military options, of which there were several a year previously, had literally been reduced to either all-out war or withdrawal from the east bank.

On the 12th July US Assistant Secretary of State Joseph Sisco disclosed that the Soviet Union had recently been shipping amphibious equipment to Egypt, and that the balance of power had been affected by more direct Soviet involvement, but he declined to say whether America would supply Israel with the asked for aircraft. On the 15th Moshe Dayan told the Knesset that the Soviet Union had increased its participation in the Egyptian air defence system, and confirmed that Soviet pilots continued to fly over Egypt. On the 31st July a cholera outbreak was reported in Egypt and all troop movement between Cairo and Alexandria was halted, some 1,500 cases being confirmed.

On the 17th July President Nasser had returned from the Soviet Union, having been persuaded to accept the risks connected with his endorsement of the second Rogers peace initiative, but the joint communiqué stated that both governments agreed that there could be no peace until the Israelis withdrew from the occupied territories. On the 20th President Nixon told a press conference that 'As far as the Soviet Union and the United States are concerned, both of us want to avoid confrontation, and that is the reason why America has not announced any sales of aircraft to Israel'. Although the high crescendo of the thunder of guns and bombs continued unabatingly, a cease fire was fast approaching over the Canal.

On the 22nd July Mahmoud Riad, the Egyptian Foreign Minister, nominally accepted the Rogers peace plan, and on the 23rd President Nasser in a broadcast speech declared his acceptance also. The peace plan was based on the November Resolution, involving Israeli withdrawal from the occupied territories and Arab recognition of Israel, and there was to be a cease fire for three months. The Israeli agreement was not so prompt or smooth. On the 28th it caused a rift within the coalition Government, even though Moshe Dayan said that Israel was sufficiently strong to compromise as long as concessions did not affect national interests. On the 31st Israel accepted the Rogers peace plan in principle, and on the 4th August

Israeli Ambassador Rabin, in Washington, gave formal acceptance to Joseph Sisco. Premier Meir had stated that Israel would participate in the discussions without any prior conditions, upon which six Gahal ministers withdrew from the Government.

On the previous day, the 3rd, U Thant and Secretary of State William Rogers had talks with Gunnar Jarring, who was brought back into the Middle East negotiations, and on the 5th the Big Four gave their approval at the UN to the Jarring peace mission. On the 7th August 1970, at 2200 hours (local time), a cease fire came into effect in the Canal Zone, but hard action continued right up to the last minutes. The Israelis, for example, alleged 194 'incidents' during the last week of the electronic war. There was to be a 'standstill' of all weapon and troop movements within 50 kilometres on either side of the Canal, both agreeing not to bring in extra arms or men.

The Israelis quote their casualties in the electronic war as 346 killed and about 3,000 wounded, but their several sets of figures tend to vary. They estimate that the Egyptians suffered at least 10,000 casualties, of whom about 2,000 were killed. They point out that the Egyptians also had a 750,000-sized refugee problem on their hands. The Egyptians (as yet) have not issued figures that make any sense. Between June 1967 and the 7th August 1970, the Israelis claim, the Egyptians lost 110 planes, against an admitted loss of 16 Israeli aircraft, of which at least six were brought down by missiles. The number of SAM sites destroyed is incalculable because of new constructions, repairs, abandonments and dummy sites, as were the number of missiles and shells fired and bombs dropped. During the last six weeks of the fighting, the brief 'electronic summer', the antagonists were more evenly matched than previously, and in this period both lost about the same number of aircraft—about half-a-dozen.

9 · The Unfought Round

'Electronics in warfare have come to stay'

When the cease fire suddenly, and to some unexpectedly, came into effect on the 7th August, both sides were tensed and ready for the 'second round', both having received the latest sophisticated weapons and counters, and both were confident of winning it. The Egyptians had received more improved SAM-2s and SAM-3s, complete with supporting radar equipment, much of which had yet to be tested in battle. These were being deployed forward, while another batch of Egyptian pilots, fresh from training in the Soviet Union, had just returned to Egypt. America had sent the Israelis at least another 200 ECM pods of the latest model; these caused a light to come on in the pilot's cabin warning him that an enemy missile had been launched and was directed towards him, enabling him to 'jam' and take evasive action; the radar automatically transmitted a flow of 'counter signals', tuned in to Russian frequencies, to distort their 'radar beams'.

Although the cease fire suspended the 'second round' the Egyptians blatantly ignored the 'military standstill' condition, and at once began moving SAMs and other weapons and equipment towards the Canal so that the 'slant range' of the missiles would completely deprive the Bar-Lev Line of aerial cover. There had been 16 operational SAM batteries in the SAM box on the 7th August, only one of which was a SAM-3. It soon became obvious that there was considerable movement of SAMs within the cease-fire zone. Although the Israelis frantically complained that the Egyptians were moving weaponry into the restricted area, both the UN and the USA hoped that it was simply a case of the SAMs already there merely being reshuffled or redeployed.

Only five days after the cease fire, on the 12th August, the Israeli Government complained to U Thant, the UN Secretary-General, about the breaches. On the 23th Moshe Dayan told the Knesset that at least six SAM launchers had been moved into the military 'standstill' zone. On the 16th US Defence Secretary Melvin Laird said that it was difficult to prove or disprove the Israeli allegations, even though on the 17th a US Defence Department spokesman admitted that US planes were carrying out reconnaissance flights along the Suez Canal. On the 19th the Americans acknowledged that 'there had been a forward deployment of Egyptian missiles by the Egyptians'. Middle East peace talks between Gunnar Jarring and the ambassadors of Egypt, Jordan and Israel did not begin until the 25th August at the UN headquarters in New York. They soon foundered, America and Israel pulling out.

On the 1st September US officials stated they were satisfied that the Egyptians were breaking cease fire conditions. On the 3rd Premier Meir said that her Government had a 'difficult argument' with America over the facts of the violations. In Israel generally there was a feeling that they had been wrongly persuaded to trust American guarantees so implicitly and to accept the conditions of the Rogers peace plan. It became increasingly obvious that the Egyptians were rushing SAMs into the cease fire zone to construct a solid SAM box, a firm barrier, that was slowly creeping towards the Canal. This was confirmed by a report on the 5th September,[1] which stated that 45 missile sites had been constructed within the cease fire zone since the 7th August, of which 30 had been armed since the cease fire, making some 270 missile launchers in this zone in all. On the 11th an Israeli spokesman claimed that there were 90 missile sites in the cease fire zone, and that the first SAM-3s had moved in.

During the weeks immediately succeeding the cease fire quantities of modern Soviet arms poured into Egypt, which included the new quadruple-barrelled ZSU 23×4 radar-controlled anti-aircraft gun, mounted on a tracked vehicle and capable of firing 4,000 rounds per minute. Formerly seen only in the Soviet Union and Poland, it was regarded as the best Soviet weapon against low-flying aircraft. On the 28th August an Egyptian military spokesman admitted that the Soviet Union had supplied Egypt with ZSU 23×4s and other arms. The other arms included a few SAM-4s, which had 'dual launchers' mounted on tracked vehicles, also making their first

[1] Institute for Strategic Studies.

appearance outside the Warsaw Pact countries. Other weapons included the Soviet heavy 203mm gun, and among other equipment were amphibious craft and vehicles.

During September 1970 a civil war blew up in Jordan, lasting from the 17th to the 27th, between King Hussein's Government and the Fedayeen. President Nasser personally mediated, and his Cairo agreement brought about a cease fire that occurred in time to save the Fedayeen temporarily from extinction in that country. On the 28th September 1970 Nasser suddenly died of a heart attack, his last political role and task being those of the peacemaker. On the 5th October Anwar Sadat was unanimously nominated President-designate by the central committee of the ASU; on the 7th the National Assembly endorsed this, and on the 22nd he was elected President of Egypt. On the 23rd Mahmoud Fawzi[1] became Premier.

On the 6th October Foreign Minister Mahmoud Riad said that Egypt would not agree to a provisional cease fire being turned into a permanent one, but on the 19th President Sadat stated his agreement to another single and final 90-day extension of the cease fire on condition that the Jarring talks were resumed, but the Israelis would not return to them. Even so, on the 6th November a second 90-day cease fire period began.

The Soviet Union increased its military support to Egypt. On the 10th October an Israeli military spokesman stated that there were over 1,000 Soviet troops manning SAM-3s within the cease fire zone, and that of the 20 missile sites set up since the 7th August five were SAM-3 installations, each requiring a minimum of 200 men to operate and guard them. On the 26th Major-General Aharon Yariv, the Israeli Director of Military Intelligence, said that the Soviet and Egyptian defences along the Suez Canal formed 'one of the most advanced missile systems in the world', adding that there were between 500 and 600 missiles along the west bank. On the same day Premier Meir stated that just before the cease fire four Soviet-piloted aircraft had been shot down by Israelis.

On the 3rd December an Israeli military spokesman said that in addition to the 13,000 Soviet personnel in Egypt and the 3,000 in the Canal Zone, there were also 'several dozen' Russian generals who had set up a headquarters capable of taking limited action without consulting Moscow, and that their staff formed a command system

[1] Not to be confused with General Mohammed Fawzi.

able to control large Soviet forces should they be air-lifted to Egypt. A consensus of reports indicated that by the end of the year there were still 200 Soviet pilots flying 150 MiG-21Js over Egypt, that the Soviet Union had gained complete control over six airfields, that there were between 12,000 and 15,000 Soviet personnel manning between 75 and 85 SAM-3 sites, with an additional 4,000 Soviet technicians servicing equipment, and that there were also about 150 Soviet Luna surface-to-surface missiles, having a range of up to 40 miles, deployed on the west bank.

Blatant disregard of the cease fire conditions that called for a 'military standstill' caused America to resume military supplies to Israel. The *New York Times* of the 24th October stated that the USA had agreed to send to Israel 180 M-48 Patton tanks as part of a $500-million arms credit programme. On the 15th November a US State Department spokesman confirmed that Israel was to receive an extra 18 Skyhawks, and that so far Israel had had 88 Skyhawks and 70 Phantoms.

While in general there was no shooting across the Canal, there were occasional incidents of minor friction that tended to increase. For example, on the 23rd November the Israelis accused the Egyptians of sending three flights of SU-7s over the east bank; on the 1st December an Israeli naval patrol vessel sank an Egyptian motor launch in the Gulf of Suez, alleging that it was engaged in intelligence work and smuggling hashish; on the 4th occurred the first armed clash since the 7th August, when Israelis killed an Egyptian soldier of a patrol that had crossed the Canal to the east bank in the southern sector; on the last day of the electronic year of 1970 the Egyptians announced that their armed forces had just completed a seven-day exercise simulating an opposed Canal crossing and a break-through into the Sinai.

Nasser's war of attrition was his last war and he intended it to be a conventional one, but it had developed beyond his control into an escalating electronic war, which he dreaded as he felt that the Americans would out-class the Russians in this field. A keen but unsuccessful exponent of conventional warfare, once the character of the struggle changed unexpectedly in 1970 Nasser became far more successful than he had ever been in the military field before, forcing the Israeli air force from the skies of Egypt and confining it to the narrow Canal Zone. This point reached, Nasser—negotiating from a position of strength, as he boasted he would—agreed to the cease fire, unpopular though it was in the Arab world which clamoured for continued military action against Israel.

Had there not been a cease fire when there was it can only be a matter of speculation how the 'second round' would have gone. With the great weight of Soviet weaponry and numbers of personnel, unless the Americans continued and increased their military aid to Israel the Israelis might have had to fall back from the Bar-Lev Line which, deprived of aerial cover, would have been subjected to intense and heavy bombardments from aircraft, missiles and guns. In such circumstances the Israelis could either have constructed a Maginot Line to withstand the pounding, which, of course, could be outflanked, or withdraw back into the Sinai. It would have been a constant question in the minds of the general staff exactly when would be the most advantageous moment to withdraw into the sprawling Bir Gifgafa ridge, when rigid linear defence could be abandoned, and allow the Israelis to revert to mobile warfare, at which they were so adept. If the 'second round' had been fought, Soviet personnel would obviously have been heavily involved and it can only be a matter of conjecture whether their involvement would have ignited World War III. Somehow one does not think this would have been the case, as the practical, hard-headed Soviet Government would, as usual wanting the fruits of war but not war itself, only go so far.

In searching for lessons to be learned, new strategy forged or new tactics evolved, apart from the electronic ones there do not seem to be any. In fact, except for a far more liberal use of concrete in place of sandbags, the scene—the linear defences on either side of the Canal, the heavy barrages and raids across the narrow strip of 'no man's water'—reminded one of trench warfare in World War I. As regards conventional defences against aircraft raids and in the initial stages of aircraft attacks, there was little that had not been amply demonstrated in World War II. Also, apart from the use of helicopters by the Israelis, the commando (including deep-penetration) raids used tactical concepts evolved in World War II. The Suez Canal effectively separated the two opposing ground forces, and in most respects it was a bloody stalemate, as in Flanders some 50 years previously but in miniature.

Egyptian military policy, as vaguely formulated by Nasser on many occasions, was to prepare for the day when Egyptian armed forces would storm the Bar-Lev Line and its armoured formations would sweep across the Sinai, driving the Israelis before them to seize and occupy Tel Aviv—a policy that was continued by President Sadat. Behind the comparative security of the waterway barrier, Nasser was able, with Soviet help, to rebuild his army, which by the time of the cease fire numbered about 650,000 men and consisted basically of three armoured, four mechanized infantry and five infantry divisions.

The quality of the 16 Egyptian artillery brigades, the majority of which were almost constantly in action, was high, but as most of the guns were 'towed' instead of being on tracks and so completely mobile, and were in concrete protected bunkers (owing to Israeli aerial assaults), a static complex developed amongst the gunners. The really sharp tip of the rather flaccid Egyptian spear was the 20 units of commandos, the men being well-trained, aggressive and capable, and they had many more successes than the Israelis would admit.

The morale of the Egyptian armed forces slowly rose after the June defeat in 1967. Within two years it had reached a high standard, after which it tended to fluctuate, usually according to the political situation and lack of promised activity. During 1970 Egyptian morale generally rose again. Throughout there had been an element of younger officers thirsting for action, and as the efficiency and capability of their units increased they became impatient, but the major part of the Egyptian army remained untested in battle. The courage of those who were in the thick of the battle, such as the gunners and the infantry at the front, was extremely commendable. In 1970, when the Israeli pilots were desperately trying to eliminate the SAM box, the bravery and fortitude of the Egyptians (and one supposes the Russians too) in immediately re-establishing SAM sites and radar overnight have obviously not been sufficiently recognized.

The Israelis and the Western press spoke slightingly of the Egyptian pilots, commenting upon their inferiority and pointing out that the Egyptians lost 110 planes to their mere 16. But this does not tell the full story. For a long time the Egyptian pilots were generally inferior to their Israeli counterparts in machines, skill and experience, but this knowledge did not prevent many of them tackling the Israelis in combat regardless of their disadvantages and losses. We have seen a 'sit down' strike of Egyptian pilots, protesting at not being allowed to take to the air and fight, at a time when Egyptian policy was to conserve, and not risk, aircraft. Owing to the electronic situation, during the last weeks of the war, Egyptian and Israeli pilots were more evenly matched, when both lost about the same number of planes.

The skill, daring and competence of the Israeli armed forces have been frequently commented upon, and indeed they are of a high order, but morale, especially of the infantry, has tended to vary, particularly in the depressing tours of duty in the Bar-Lev Line. To an army trained for mobile offensive action, whose sole form of defence until 1967 was to attack, the role of static defence was a new one, at the best a tedious drag and an unwelcome chore. In time of war it was always the policy of the Israelis to put their best formations into action first, and then progressively to use brigades not quite so well trained or equipped in their order of capability. In the June War many Israeli brigades, especially the infantry ones, saw no action at all, but the élite formations saw plenty. Manning the Bar-Lev Line was a duty that fell to the infantry, and usually two infantry brigades, sometimes three, were involved. Armoured formations lay back a few miles from the Canal in support ready to beat back any landing attempt, as did the gunners who, with their mobile guns, came forward at intervals to fire and then withdraw again. Therefore, while one would not doubt that the armoured brigades retained their mobile offensive thinking and morale, as had the paratroops who were mainly used for commando raids, one might question what effect this war had on the Israeli infantry, which comprises 22 of the 31 brigades Israel is able to muster in an emergency.

In essence it was primarily a Soviet-Egyptian war, as although Egypt provided the setting, most of the resources and manpower, the Soviet contribution in the form of aircraft, missiles, weaponry, technicians, soldiers and pilots was huge. Although other Arab nations clamoured for an all-out war against Israel, and urged Nasser on, few gave him any practical assistance and fewer still sent soldiers to fight with him. Only Libya, the Sudan, Algeria and Kuwait sent detachments of troops to the Suez Canal Zone. Perhaps because of political reasons the PLA brigade stationed in the Canal Zone seemed to be completely inactive. The Israelis retained the advantage that they fought against an uneasy, divided, hesitant and distrustful coalition of Arab states.

Coming finally to the electronic aspect of this war, which marks its importance in history and lifts it from the rut of shambling military conventionality, it cannot be disputed that the two super powers used this small Middle East cockpit to battle-test their electronic equipment. Had both powers withheld aircraft, weapons and all military aid, this electronic war would not and could not have been fought. Both America and the Soviet Union must have gained great electronic experience, expertise and vital research information, that will contribute to their own military capabilities, which they would not have otherwise obtained. Much electronic detail of a military nature that is freely available in scientific journals is too technical to be quoted or explained to the general reader. There must, of course, be a vast amount more that remains classified.

An examination of the electronic war, really the first in history, leaves me with four main deductions. The first is that, as in any other form of warfare, progress in sophistication of weaponry and equipment is inevitable, and that for every electronic advance that brings an advantage to one side or the other a counter will be sought and eventually found. We saw the progressions in effectiveness in the American ECM pods. The second deduction is that electronic warfare is a highly specialized subject, requiring specialized training and special aptitudes to develop the battle techniques of jamming, counter-jamming, deception and avoidance, and so yet another specialist element had to be added to armies, making them even more complex. The third deduction is that missile belts or screens need not be static as was often the case when anti-aircraft guns were defending a fixed site, but they can move forward, and in doing so (unless, of course, neutralized by ECMs), can with their 'slant range' deprive the enemy ahead of his aerial cover and support. Large formations can have their own integral missile belts, both for protection and as an aid to the attack, as SAMs can be mounted on tracked vehicles for mobility. The Egyptians were just moving into this stage, having relied upon static, 'concrete circle' missile launcher sites almost until the cease fire, but immediately afterwards their SAM box 'advanced' towards the Suez Canal, and the Israelis could do nothing about it. The fourth deduction is that as yet electronics cannot entirely replace men; for example, they cannot sufficiently differentiate between friendly and enemy aircraft on a radar screen. The Egyptian aircraft remained high overhead and did not swoop to attack Israeli planes until the missile system had been switched off. Switching the missile system on and off requires split-second timing, and one guesses that the Egyptians, and perhaps also the Israelis, must have lost aircraft downed by their own missile or anti-aircraft fire, as have other nations in war.

Electronic warfare made an immense advance in Nasser's war of attrition, which firmly put it on the map, and further advances are inevitable. It cannot be so long before we enter the age of 'war by electronics', when pilotless aircraft will attack missile systems operated automatically, there being no personnel immediately involved in the battle area. We may look forward to a war in which machines and electronic equipment are the main casualties, and not personnel, as they might be fought at a distance by technicians in uniform rather than soldiers in close combat. One must end by concluding that electronics in warfare have come to stay and their degree of involvement will only be limited by the wealth, resources and technical capability of the country concerned, or its ability, like that of Egypt and Israel, to persuade larger nations to supply them with electronic military means.

Appendix A

Brief Chronology of the Electronic War

1967

5-10 June	The third Arab-Israeli war, also referred to as the Six Day War, in which the Egyptians were beaten back to the Suez Canal by the Israelis.
20 June	Soviet Chief of Staff visits Egypt.
21 June	Soviet President visits Egypt.
25 June	First planeload of Soviet arms arrives in Egypt.
1 July	Egyptian commandos attempt to cross Suez Canal.
3 July	Israelis admit first act of sabotage in the Sinai.
5 July	Two Israeli officers killed by Egyptian mortar fire.
8 July	Israelis lose five killed and 31 wounded by Egyptian shelling.
12 July	Israelis sink two Egyptian MTBs.
14 July	First heavy Egyptian artillery barrage across the Canal.
30 August	(to 3 September) Khartoum Conference.
14 September	Suicide of Marshal Amer.
21 October	Egyptians sink Israeli destroyer *Eilat*.
24 October	Israeli artillery and mortar barrages destroy two oil refineries at Port Suez.
22 November	The United Nations 'November Resolution' Number 242.
23 November	Nasser's bellicose speech.
3 December	General Bar-Lev appointed Israeli Chief of Staff.

1968

February	Student riots in Cairo and Helwan.
July	Nasser to Moscow to ask for more arms.

October	Israelis commence fortifying the Bar-Lev Line.
8 October	Israel presents peace plan to the UN.
26 October	Egyptian 'Mitla Pass' operation: heaviest shelling so far.
30 October	The Nag Hamadi raid—first Israeli commando deep-penetration raid into Egypt.
November	Student riots in Egypt.
16 November	National Defence Council set up in Egypt.
28 December	Israeli commandos raid Beirut airport.

1969

4 February	Yassir Arafat appointed Chairman of the Palestine Liberation Organization (PLO).
24 February	State of emergency declared in Egypt.
26 February	Death of Israeli Premier Levi Eshkol.
27 February	Nasser visits troops in the Canal Zone.
6 March	Heavy Egyptian artillery barrages across the Canal begin.
7 March	Mrs Golda Meir appointed Israeli Premier.
9 March	Egyptian Chief of Staff, General Riad, killed by Israeli shell at front;
	Nation-wide 'black-out' decreed in Egypt;
	Israeli Piper Cub plane brought down by SAM-2.
27 March	War of attrition begins: Nasser's speech to the Arab Socialist Union (ASU).
29 April	Second Israeli reprisal raid into the Upper Nile Valley.
24 May	Israeli HAWK missile brings down Egyptian MiG-21 for first time.
29 June	Third Israeli commando raid into the Upper Nile Valley.
1 July	Israeli Premier Meir utters biblical threat.
7 July	U Thant speaks of 'open war along the Canal'.
19 July	Israelis raid Green Island.
20 July	First Egyptian air raids into Israeli-held territory. First aerial combats.
	This Egyptian challenge to the Israeli air force lasted two weeks.

27 July	Swedish UN observer killed.
9 September	Israelis mount their 'ten hour war'.
	A senior Soviet military adviser killed.
11 September	102 Egyptian aircraft raided into the Sinai.
September	Israeli air force begins to bomb SAM and radar sites.
28 October	Rogers peace initiative (made public on 9 December).
October	Israeli air force begins to destroy the Egyptian early warning system.
8 November	Egyptian naval raid on Romani.
6 December	Exchange of prisoners: two Israelis for 58 Egyptians.
18 December	Egyptian Defence Minister to Moscow to ask for more arms.
22 December	Israel rejects Rogers peace initiative.
23 December	Soviet Union rejects Rogers peace initiative.
25 December	Five French-built gunboats manned by Israelis slip out of Cherbourg harbour—to arrive in Israel on the 31st.
27 December	Israeli commandos raid Ras Ghaleb and seize a new Soviet P-12 radar system.

1970

7 January	First Israeli deep-penetration bombing raid.
22 January	Israelis raid Shadwan Island.
	Nasser to Moscow to ask for more sophisticated arms.
5 February	Egyptian frogmen damage two Israeli ships in Eilat harbour.
6 February	Israeli aircraft sink Egyptian minelayer.
12 February	Israelis bomb factory at Abu Zambal.
14 March	Israeli commandos land on west bank of Canal.
18 March	Reports of SAM-3s arriving in Egypt.
23 March	Israelis begin attacking the SAM box from air.
end of March	Reports of new MiG-21Js, with Soviet pilots, arriving in Egypt.
Beginning of April	Soviet pilots flying defensive missions over Nile Valley.

8 April	Israelis bomb Egyptian school.
13 April	Last Israeli deep-penetration raid.
May	Egyptians construct new SAM box.
1 May	Speech by Nasser marks his re-emergence as a confident leader.
3 May	Egyptian commandos fire rockets at Israeli-held El Tor.
4 May	Egyptian planes raid El Arish.
13 May	Israeli fishing boat sunk by Egyptians.
16 May	Israeli aircraft sink Egyptian destroyer and Komar Class missile boat.
19 May	Egyptian commando raid in strength across Canal.
28 May	Eight-day aerial assault on Port Said begins.
25 June	US Secretary of State Rogers announces his second peace initiative.
29 June	Nasser to Moscow (remains until 17th July).
29/30 June	Improved SAM-2s moved towards Canal: Israelis suddenly lose three aircraft.
19 July	Israelis lose fourth Phantom aircraft to SAMs.
23 July	Nasser accepts the Rogers peace plan.
4 August	Israel accepts the Rogers peace plan.
5 August	Big Four at UN approve the Jarring peace mission.
7 August	Ceasefire across the Suez Canal for three months: 'military standstill' within 50 kilometres of the Canal itself.

Appendix B

UN Security Council Resolution of 22nd November 1967

The Security Council, Expressing its continuing concern with the grave situation in the Middle East,

Emphasizing the inadmissibility of the acquisition of territory by war and the need to work for a just and lasting peace in which every State in the area can live in security.

Emphasizing further that all member States in the acceptance of the Charter of the United Nations have undertaken a commitment to act in accordance with Article 2 of the Charter,

1. Affirms that the fulfilment of Charter principles requires the establishment of a just and lasting peace in the Middle East which should include the application of both the following principles:

I Withdrawal of Israeli armed forces from territories occupied in the recent conflict;

II Termination of all claims or states of belligerency and respect for and acknowledgement of the sovereignty, territorial integrity and political independence of every State in the area and their right to live in peace within secure and recognized boundaries free from threats or acts of force.

2. Affirms further the necessity

A. For guaranteeing freedom of navigation through international waters in the area;

B. For achieving a just settlement of the refugee problem;

C. For guaranteeing the territorial inviolability and political independence of every State in the area, through measures including the establishment of demilitarized zones.

3. Requests the Secretary-General to designate a special representative to proceed to the Middle East to establish and maintain contacts with the States concerned in order to promote agreement and assist

efforts to achieve a peaceful and accepted settlement in accordance with the provisions and principles in this resolution.

4. Requests the Secretary-General to report to the Security Council on the progress of the efforts of the special representatives as soon as possible.

Index

The following words are not included in the Index as they appear on the majority of the pages of the book: Arab(s); Egypt(ian)(s); Israel(i)(s); Middle East; Gamal Abdul Nasser; Suez Canal (Zone).